Musings OF A MENOPAUSAL INSOMNIAC

Crazy, Dog Lady

Musings of a Menopausal Insomniac Crazy, Dog Lady

Suzie de Jonge

Published by The Kind Press in 2025
thekindpress.com

Text copyright © Suzie de Jonge 2025
All rights reserved.
No part of this publication may be reproduced without prior written permission from the publisher.

A catalogue record for this book is available from the National Library of Australia.

ISBN: 9781763800915 (paperback)

Cover Artwork by Gemma Correll, gemmacorrell.com
No reproduction or use of illustrations without permission.
Cover layout and typeset by Nicola Matthews

We at The Kind Press acknowledge that Aboriginal and Torres Strait Islander peoples are the Traditional Custodians and the first storytellers of the lands on which we live and work; and we pay our respects to Elders past and present.

DISCLAIMER: The content presented in this book is meant for inspiration and information purposes only. The purchaser of this book understands that the author is not a medical professional, and the information contained within this book is not intended to replace medical advice or to be relied upon to treat, cure or prevent any disease, illness or medical condition. It is understood that you will seek full medical clearance by a licenced physician before making any changes mentioned in this book. The author and publisher claim no responsibility to any person or entity for any liability, loss or damage caused or alleged to be caused directly or indirectly as a result of the use, application or interpretation of the material in this book. Some names, locations and identifying characteristics of individuals in this book have been changed to protect the privacy of those depicted.

*To my darling Daisy Girl,
we love you more than sunshine*

CONTENTS

Foreword		*xi*
Chapter 1	The sleep cycle of a menopausal, insomniac, crazy dog lady (OR the wake cycle more like)	1
Chapter 2	Musings of an everyday woman on internet dating in the 2020s (OR we are not in Kansas anymore, Dorothy!)	9
Chapter 3	The good, bad and the ugly of living on your own (OR the things 'they' never tell you)	25
Chapter 4	All creatures great and small (OR for the love of God, why?)	37
Chapter 5	What cheddars me off (OR enough already)	49
Chapter 6	Life begins at forty – Part One: What NOT to Wear	61
Chapter 7	Life begins at forty – Part Two: The wheels on the bus … fall off	75

Chapter 8	Things my mother told me (OR 'because I said so')	89
Chapter 9	The undomestic goddess	97
Chapter 10	Is it just me or …?	109
Chapter 11	The rhythm of the night (at 14 Woody Views Way)	121
Chapter 12	My chequered history with exercise of the physical kind (OR exercise is my kryptonite)	131
Chapter 13	Mr and Mrs MICDL's excellent adventure – Part One: Planes, trains and automobiles	143
Chapter 14	Mr and Mrs MICDL's excellent adventure – Part Two: Men are from Venus, women are from Mars 91	159
Chapter 15	Thelma and Louise (AKA Daisy and Maggie)	165
Chapter 16	Men-o-pause (OR It's getting hot in here!)	175

Afterword   *189*
Acknowledgements   *191*
About the Author   *194*

FOREWORD

I don't know if I would call this a *'book'* per se. I think I would describe it more as a collection of what I call my *'musings'*; random pieces I have written about living in the world, as I see it through my eyes.

And who am I? If I had to describe myself, I would probably say a kind of odd, quirky, nerdy, middle-aged woman, who makes it her mission in life to be kind to others, but who also doesn't take herself too seriously, loves humour as it makes her world go around and, also, of course, a menopausal, insomniac, crazy dog lady (MICDL for short). Welcome to my world!

To explain the flow of these musings, it is necessary for me to share a little personal background. When I first started putting pen to paper, I was going through some big changes in my life, which included sorting out my head and heart, and for the first time ever, at the age of fifty-something, experiencing living life on my own.

Hence, the chapters at the beginning of this book are focused on certain aspects of my life at that time. Fast forward a couple of years, and as the Universe follows its own divinely designated path, I reunited with my partner. We are now once again happily ensconced in our little bubble of marital bliss (not sure if these are exactly the words he would personally use, but he's not writing this book, so he doesn't get a say!). Therefore, the remainder of the chapters in the book are written during this latter period.

Luckily for Mr MICDL, he is used to my idiosyncrasies, my total lack of direction and awareness of my surroundings or powers of observation, my inability to refold a pizza box or a fitted sheet and my absolute (apparently) inability to park my car in the garage the way he particularly likes it.

Me, I am used to his inability to sit still for more than ten minutes, his need for perfect order (I don't complain about this one, especially as it involves him doing housework), his snoring and his sometimes lack of patience with me, our pups and random strangers.

One of the things I enjoy the most about our union, however, is absolutely the way we can just laugh together, be silly and bounce our silliness off one another. Mr MICDL calls it our *'banter'*. Sometimes, I think that if people overheard us, we would sound like a corny British comedy duo (think '*The Two Ronnies*'). Therefore, I am grateful we are a match made in a very peculiar heaven.

But honestly, where would our lives be without humour? Humour has gotten me, and I am sure many people out there, through some very difficult times. It has helped me to not take life or myself too seriously. It has given me a different perspective, and most of all it has brought me joy. There is even proven science stuff, that laughter releases endorphins (the *'happy'* hormones) into our system and makes us instantly feel better. Well, if it's *proven science stuff*, it can't be wrong, can it?

My ultimate wish for you, though, my dear reader, is to bring a smile to your face, maybe even a laugh or a snort out loud and, most importantly, fill you with good feelings.

Enjoy!

The sleep cycle of a menopausal, insomniac, crazy dog lady (OR the wake cycle more like)

So, the fateful time has come for the long walk up the stairs to my bedroom. Most people think of their bedroom as a peaceful sanctuary and look forward to it. Me? Yeah, nuh, not so much. I would honestly pay a million dollars to be able to sleep right through the night, something that a lot of people just take for granted. Not so for this MICDL.

Ah, yes, and whose great idea was it to have my dogs (aka *The Girls*) sleep in the bedroom with me? That would be me, of course!

The period Mr MICDL and I spent apart resulted in the uprooting of my two foofy daughters from the only home they had ever known. Consequently, I was concerned they would fret in new surroundings and miss their two-legged dad. So, feeling guilty, I let them sleep in my bedroom, just for a few nights I thought. Well, that was a good move, wasn't it? … Um no, not so much in hindsight. After only a few nights of them being in my bedroom with me, I decided it was time to reestablish my previously held boundaries and shut the door at bedtime to sleep on my own. However, this resulted in much crying and scratching at the door and, feeling even guiltier, I weakened and let them in, just to try to grab some crumbs of sleep. Hence, as the saying goes, I made my bed and literally ... had to lie in it.

Let's add menopause and insomnia into the mix just for fun. Why not! A typical night usually goes like this.

2.00 am-ish: I wake up feeling like I am self-combusting from the weight of the bed coverings, my clothes are stuck to me, my hair wet, the pillow soaked. I may throw the covers off or stick a random arm or leg out, trying to find a cool bit of sheet and thus the cycle begins.

Next, what some of us menopausal women (or at least my best friend and I) commonly refer to as the *'rotisserie chicken'* manoeuvre may come into play. This involves much tossing from one side to the other, throwing covers on, then covers off. A leg or arm may be thrust out from underneath the covers to hopefully catch a stray breeze. By this stage, one will do whatever one can to have a chance to get back to sleep. This may also involve praying to the sleep gods, or *anyone* who will listen, to grant the ever-elusive gift of sleep .

Essential oils, sleepy spray, eye mask, ear plugs, sleep meditations, hypnotherapy, prescription sleeping tablets, natural sleeping tablets, sleepy tea, hot bath before bed, exercise before bed, exercise in the morning, special pillows. *'They'* say don't eat spicy food or chocolate before going to bed, don't have caffeine too late in the day, don't do anything too stimulating, don't drink alcohol, drink alcohol! You name it ... I have tried it.

So, here I find myself once again. It's the middle of the night and my mind is spinning like a whirling dervish; a myriad of unproductive and random thoughts running through it like a track on repeat. Song lyrics stuck in my mind play over and over and over again. What am I going to cook this week? Best I put together a shopping list. Also, I must remember to do x, y, and z when I get up in the morning. Or, perhaps I may analyse the movie I watched the night before, picking holes in the plot. They forgot to tie up that loose end and what happened to that character?

I hear every noise like it's amplified. The whirring of the fan, the fridge motor turning on and off downstairs in the kitchen, the hum of traffic from the motorway, someone doing wheelies in the next street, bats screeching as they fly by, a dog barking, the crackling of the power lines. There are also the visuals that sneak through my closed eyelids, the stupid vertical blinds that let in cracks of streetlight or a full moon, or lying there waiting for the light to flash on the smoke alarm attached to the ceiling.

Everything annoys me. My pyjama legs are riding up. I'm too hot. I'm too cold. A stray wisp of hair tickles my face. My ear is crumpled under my head. There is a wrinkle in the sheet beneath me.

Visualise walking down ten steps, they say *('them'* again!), and you will drift off. Yeah, right. After going up and down those stupid steps half a dozen times, I'd say I can safely debunk that theory for catering to my particular sleep challenges.

Let's add into the mix a twenty-eight-kilogram dog the size of a small pony, who insists on sharing my bed. I can only describe this as being similar to sleeping with a toddler who has consumed an inordinate amount of sugary fizzy drink. As I am just starting to drift off, feeling that letting-go feeling, maybe with an inadvertent jerk of the body signalling I'm going into *the sleep zone*, Miss Maggie Bear will stand up on the bed, do a few turns around and drop back down on the bed with a thud, on the exact same spot she was originally on, finished off with a loud sigh. This will occur numerous times a night, along with a mixture of yips, smacking of her chops and twitching in her sleep, whilst dreaming about Lord only knows what.

Then there is her snoring. Sleeping with this dog is like sleeping with a grown man with sleep apnoea. I nudge her or even call out her name to wake her. It may stop for a minute or two. Yay, I silently cheer and … it starts up again, even louder. So, of course, me being me, I lie there anticipating the next snore. When I slept with Mr MICDL, a gold-medal-award-winning snorer, I had what I call the *'Rule of Three'*. If I needed to nudge him three times to stop the snoring and that didn't work, off to the spare room I went. I can't believe I am contemplating that because of a dog!

After about two hours of this nightly ritual, I may finally start drifting off again. I stretch my legs out to get comfortable and … for the love of God! I get a crippling cramp in my calf or foot. Of course, rubbing it doesn't help, so I have to get up and hobble around my bedroom until it eases. I might as well go to the bathroom while I'm up, I think. So, I kill two birds with one stone and stumble back to bed, by this time, as wide awake as when I initially got into bed.

Rinse and repeat.

When I eventually wake up in the morning, after finally managing to snatch a few broken hours' sleep, I usually have a pillow over my head to block out the snores and other external noises, along with my earphones virtually strangling me. As soon as I stir and open my eyes, I'm looking straight into the loving face of my furry daughter Miss Maggie Bear, close enough to me that I can feel her warm doggy breath. Now she realises I am awake, there is no lying around—it's breakfast time, Mum!

Ms Maggie Bear and her morning face.

When I drag myself out of bed to start the day and look in the mirror, I see a crumpled, tired face looking back at me, with hair that looks remarkably like I have stuck my finger in a power socket. I smile back at her. Congratulations, you have made it through another night! Woo hoo!

Musings of an everyday woman on internet dating in the 2020s (OR we are not in Kansas anymore, Dorothy!)

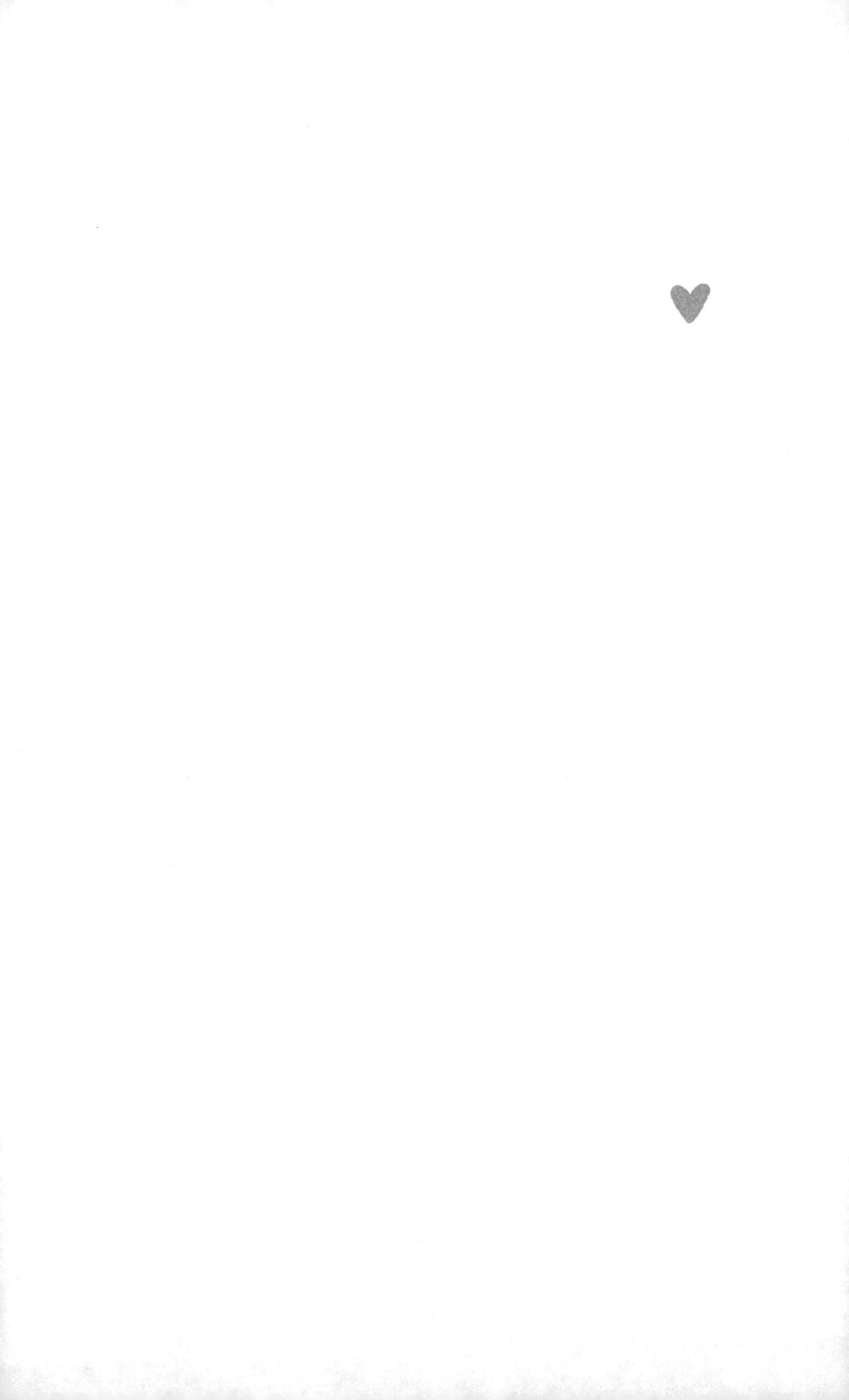

I never thought I would again enter the somewhat bizarre and surreal world of internet dating on the wrong side of fifty-five, but a while back, this is where I found myself. We all need to connect with others on some level. It is an innate part of our makeup as human beings, and that calling was making itself known to me. Yes, being single and living on my own has its huge advantages, like eating when and what I like, watching my fluffy shows on TV and being able to take up the whole bed (to name a few), but there is nothing quite like finding that person I truly want to be with and look forward to seeing, who feels the same way about me.

So, how do you meet people in this era, apart from hanging out at a bar, joining a Singles Meet Up Group with like-minded, like-aged people (tried that and failed miserably—I didn't know it was possible to fail at that but apparently it is!), or hoping that Mr Right might randomly find you and come knock on your front door?

I had dabbled in online dating about some twenty years ago, when the internet was first born. It was before I met my former partner in a much more traditional and pleasant way, a blind date orchestrated by my best friend. However, it seems that things have changed mightily on the internet-dating front, and well, hmm, not so much in a great way. I know I speak for a lot of other lonely hearts out there, men and women alike. So, where do you even begin on this perilous adventure? It might be easiest if I break it down into a few steps.

Step One: Find the site you connect with (or maybe several to cast the net wider). You have your Bumble, RSVP, Tinder, eHarmony, Match.com, Silver Singles, Elite Singles, Spiritual Singles and Plenty of Fish to list just a few. You name it, there is a site for everyone. *Warning*—do your research. Some sites are not aimed at dating but are purely for *'hooking up'* (what's with all these references to fishing?).

Step Two: Put together a profile with flattering recent photos, a snappy catch line and try to make yourself seem vaguely interesting. Of course, most sites give you helpful *'hints'* on what you should and shouldn't do to make yourself *'right swipe-able'*. (I had to do a bit of research on the *'swiping'* bit. Call me naïve, but there you go). Lots of articles tell you how to do this if you google it, but the bottom line is don't say all the things you *don't* want. For example, don't say, *'Don't be a d**k, no game players, leave your baggage behind, no mind games'* as that can come across a tad off-putting to potential future mates, apparently.

While this second step may not sound difficult, it is amazing how hard it is to describe yourself and what you are looking for in 200 characters or less. It may take some time and rejigging to feel semi-comfortable that you are not describing yourself as:

(a) Miss Universe
(b) Bridget Jones, desperate and dateless

Somewhere in the middle is probably just right.

Okay, you've spent hours trying to pick the best photos you already have. Or maybe you put on your glad rags and make-up and attempted a selfie *(warning, don't attempt this if you are over fifty as you don't have selfie-taking in your DNA)*. Maybe you got a trusted friend to take some semi-decent photos of you where you don't look too stiff and ridiculous or like a deer in the headlights. And you have also mashed together some sort of bio. Now you are ready to post your profile. This is where the *'fun'* (and I use that term loosely) begins. You are ready to share your profile with the worldwide web.

You can expect to feel vulnerable, like people are judging you, but I promise you, no more than you judge the potential *'matches'* that appear in your feed or are suggested to you after you take the *'compatibility test'* some sites have.

This is the part where you may (if you are a woman) silently wonder if the profile that comes up in front of you wants to date a woman or their identical twin? Interests listed may include, but are not limited to, camping, fishing, motorbike riding, boating, football, Worldwide Wrestling, speed racing and climbing mountains. Not that there is anything wrong with any of these. I am sure some women out there may find that attractive. However, the majority of the females I know want to meet someone who has similar interests to them, which may or may not include extreme sports.

There also appears to be a double standard about what men expect of women's profile photos, as opposed to their own. I have seen many a grumble by men that a lot of women don't look like their profiles when they meet them in person but, hey guys, this is a two-way street. This direct quote came from an opening line of a profile I saw … *'Firstly, if your picture is not reasonably recent, your age, or anything else is a lie, then there's no need to read any further!!'* Love the two exclamation marks at the end of this sentence and, by the way, this guy's pictures were so blurry he could have been anyone!! *(My two exclamation marks.)*

Mr Google suggests you put photos up that are recent and not blurry. Don't include other people, don't wear sunglasses in each one and so on. Most men on these sites must have missed that particular memo.

I have seen a myriad of profile photos, and list just a sample of these below:
- Holding one or several fish.
- One or all profile photos come with sunglasses and hats on, hiding eyes and hair—or lack thereof.
- The awful obligatory selfie in the bathroom (please, put the toilet seat down if doing this and also … try harder).
- Half of the person is cut off or blurry.
- Photo taken from so far away it is impossible to make out the person.

- Photo has other men in it without pointing out which one they are (kind of like *'Where's Wally?'*).
- Photo with another woman (hopefully not someone they are currently dating or married to).
- Photo with their children.
- Photo of their children and not them.
- Photo with their mother! I kid you not, one guy, who looked like he may have belonged to the Hells Angels, had a photo of him and his elderly mother next to his Harley. I wonder if they come as a pair?
- Photos of their car, four-wheel-drive, boat, motorbike or even earth-moving equipment (with or without them in the picture).
- Their high school or wedding photo.
- Photos without a shirt (please put it back on) or trying to look sexy by lying on their bed (it is not, just saying).
- Photos where they look grumpy and are glaring at the camera (or have what I term the *'grumpy cat face'*).
- Pulling crazy faces.
- Dressed up in a fancy dress costume.

However, I'm not totally harsh. I do allow dog photos … with or without the person in it. Either is fine.

You also have your imaginative taglines, which is another first impression of a potential suitor. Again, I have listed here some direct quotes I have come across such as:
- *'Thought I'd give this internet dating thing a go and see what happens.'*

- *'Bush bear looking for his Goldilocks.'*
- *'Just another fat man dreaming the impossible dream on RSVP - been here ten years for zero so expecting nothing.'*
- *'I don't bite ... well, maybe sometimes.'*
- *'"This would be fun", they said.'*
- And finally, my all-time favourite ... *'Just pick me! Or someone who looks like me! This section is way too hard and whatever I write may or may not be true'* Boom—winner, winner, chicken dinner!

Then there are the profiles where the person lists all the things they *don't* want in a future relationship, usually a dead give-away of someone who has been burnt or hurt in a past relationship. Whilst it is totally understandable and natural for some men (and I'm sure women, too) to feel this way, airing it as the first introduction to themselves on a dating profile is not really a huge turn on for a prospective mate. Rings a few alarm bells (who am I kidding—*many* alarm bells!) when painting all of the human race with the same brush and passive aggressiveness. What is that saying? You attract more flies with honey. There are also the mystifying acronyms included in profiles, which in my naivety again, I needed to google such as:
- 420-friendly (huh?)
- NSA
- FWB
- ONS
- MBA (I thought that was a degree!)
- Poly (that one would be a HELL no!)

Some list their Myers-Briggs personality type (another thing I had to google), ESTJ, INFP, etc. I understand these people may be intellectuals and are perhaps trying to attract their similar mate, but can you just spell it out for those who may be less familiar with the world of personality tests, so we don't feel quite so ill-educated?

Warning! You also have one of the most dangerous and reproachable of profiles, your catfish (more fishing references!). These are the ones who take someone's random photos off the internet and pretend to be them. They normally have unusual names like Reynaldo or Connor, and the photo is of a silver fox, the Achilles heel for most middle-aged women, including myself. They tell you how they are humanitarians, normally an engineer or project manager of some sort, working away from their hometown of *xxx* (which, of course, is in close proximity to you). They tell you what wonderful morals and values they have, how they want to settle down and cherish someone and, of course, my darling, it could be you (this is after one conversation). After the second conversation, this escalates to them declaring their underlying love. The third, most likely, is asking you to marry them as well as lend them money (my love) to get them out of war-torn *'insert country here'* as their money is tied up in a foreign bank account, their passport has been stolen, they are in hospital or they are being illegally held in jail, so they can be with you and live happily ever after. You just have to google *'catfish'* to find many an example of some poor soul who has been fleeced out of their life savings and left with a broken heart for what they *thought* their future might have been. There is even a TV show by that name, which exposes these fishes to their unsuspecting bait and breaks tender heart by tender heart each episode.

So, if you finally find someone who you think doesn't look like a serial killer and is worth meeting, there is the obligatory *'coffee date'*. Me, I personally prefer a *'wine date'*, so that if I have made a huge mistake in judgement by their profile, I can at least drown my sorrows. Many scenarios played out like this for me, as I am sure they have for others, men and women alike. I finally get up the nerve to meet someone for a *'date'*. I walk into the venue, see a guy sitting there on his own and think, *'Hmm, that looks nothing like the guy in the picture. Please don't let it be him.'* It's like a little mantra running through my mind, *'Please God, don't let it be him. Please God, don't let it be him.'* Then said date waves at you and your stomach sinks. How old was that photo? Twenty years? In it, he had hair and no beer belly and I also thought from his profile that he was taller than me (me being five foot-ish). This is the moment when you wish the ground could just open up and swallow you whole. So as not to be rude (even though it is a challenge not to turn straight around and flee!), you sit for an obligatory coffee or drink and chit chat about nothing in particular. You make an excuse to escape—such as meeting a friend or some other specially thought-out scenario—never to be seen again. You get home and instantly unfriend or block said potential *'date'*.

However, you may have an experience after much *'swiping'* to finally meet someone who seems kind of okay. The conversation may be going alright until they start talking about their ex-partner. I have a kind of rule that if I don't know someone well, I don't think it's appropriate (or attractive) to diss your ex. Don't take your ex's inventory and share it with someone you are on a date with whom you might want to see again. A person degrading and airing their obvious bitterness is not appealing for a potential new partner. What is the phrase I am looking for? A *'turn off'* and also another alarm bell ringer! Now, to be fair, I am only stating things how I see them from a female point of view. Believe me, women may be just as guilty of this as men.

Phew, so you finally meet a person you like and think, okay, this might be something to look forward to. But after a meeting or two … crickets. They go quiet and drop off the grid. Again, in my naivety, I didn't know there is an actual term for this—ghosting. This was the most difficult thing to deal with. You start thinking it's about you, and you begin taking your own inventory. Thoughts run through your mind like …

'What is wrong with me?'
'What is it about me that this has happened again?'
'Why can't people just be honest?'

This place can be so dangerous and damaging to your self-esteem, self-confidence and self-worth. Nobody likes to be rejected. It just hurts when you are already at your most vulnerable from putting yourself out there.

It has taken me some time to realise it is not about me. It is always about the other person. I know, and I see my daughter fall into the same pattern, that we expect other people to treat us the way we treat them. This is an honest and transparent way to live our life, and the world would be a much kinder place if we all did this. But, if we do follow this somewhat idealistic philosophy, sadly, we will be hurt over and over, because that is *not,* unfortunately, how everyone thinks. The only actions you have control over are your own. This was the point I needed to look inside myself, regroup and lick my wounds. I needed to remind myself that I am unique, I am special, I am worthy and I need to love myself first, let things flow and live as though I already have that love, because I do inside myself.

I wrote a little poem and called it, *'The One Who Wins My Heart',* as a reminder to *myself* of exactly that.

> *The one who wins my heart will know it is a heart worth winning.*
>
> *They will want to know everything about me, and me about them.*
>
> *They will value my worth, as I will honour and respect their worth.*
>
> *They will realise how precious my love is and treasure it, as I will treasure their love.*
>
> *They will see me for the true me, flaws and all, and still love me, as I will love them.*

They will feel my tender heart's limitless capacity to love and hold it gently in their hands.

Love is not hard unless we make it so.

So, the moral of this story, I guess, is that we all need connection but need to connect with ourselves first, to realise that each and every one of us deserves to be loved, and to treat each other with kindness and respect.

Postscript

Life has a funny way of unfolding and, as they say, destiny is divinely guided. Sometime after writing this piece, my former partner and I started spending time together again and, unexpectedly but delightfully, reunited, for which we are both grateful and happy. It is the same but different, with the time apart letting us rediscover who we are, what is truly important to us and fall in love all over again.

This experience, however, of dipping my toes into the internet dating pool gave me another unexpected gift, the ability to re-evaluate my own self-worth and value. This was something that over the years, due to many different circumstances, had become neglected and forgotten. Sometimes we all need a little reminder to give ourselves that bit of TLC and recognition that can only come for us. I hope you, dear reader, can give this gift to yourself, too. You are worthy of that.

By the way, in case you were curious, my tagline was,

'Things I have in common with Victoria Secret models ... I'm hungry'. I was just being my quirky, sassy self and that's okay. That's who we all should be, ourselves, because you can't get that wrong. Good luck fishing!

The good, bad and the ugly of living on your own (OR the things 'they' never tell you)

♥

This last year was the first time I have ever lived on my own. You know, you may go from living with your family to living with flatmates, boyfriends, partners, partners and kids. When Mr MICDL and I decided to live apart, it was just me, my one two-legged and two four-legged daughters for a bit. Then Miss MICDL moved out to do a bit of *'adulting stuff'* of her own. For the first time in my entire life, I lived on my own in my fifty *'blah blah'* years.

It was all new and different, and me being me, I thought I would categorise the good bits and some of the challenges I had. I don't like to say *'bad'* because they're never really bad, they're just something I had never experienced before.

First of all, the good bits. Now, as any adult with kids knows, once their kids move out, it's kind of nice to walk around in different states of dress or undress without worrying about being seen or obligatory giggling or looks of abject horror that only teenage children seem to express. Being able to walk around as I please, because let's face it, the four-legged daughters don't care, gets a big tick.

Next is eating what I like, when I like and not having to put a meal on the table. Watching what I like on TV without having to see raised eyebrows at my choices. If I feel like not cleaning up, I don't have to. I don't mind time on my own. It's kind of nice to just potter and do things around the place.

Another plus is it doesn't matter what you look like in the morning. I can tell you, I certainly look a lot different when I wake up to what I share on social media and with the general public—the four-legged daughters don't judge me. That's a definite high-five moment.

So, these are some of the positive things that come to mind.

However, on the opposing team, I have noticed a few, I suppose, cons ... Maybe I will call them scenarios?

Scenario One

I have developed a habit lately, which is a tad disconcerting. I've done it a bit over the last few years, while spending more time on my own working from home. It's talking to myself out loud. Now, I tell myself I'm talking to my four-legged daughters but I'm not. Actually, I'm talking to myself, and I've noticed I am doing it an awful lot lately.

It's okay at home, I guess, though I have heard my lovely next-door neighbours having a bit of a giggle on the other side of the fence on occasions when I do it whilst in the backyard. However, I noticed I was doing it when I went to the supermarket the other day ... out loud, in public! I was discussing what I was buying, weighing up the pros and cons, when someone walked past me and gave me this weird look. Then I realised, OMG, I said that out loud, not just in my own head! I also realise how much more I am doing it. So yes, that's a bit of a worry. I might need to keep an eye on that particular emerging situation.

Scenario Two

One thing I do miss when living on my own is watching television with my two-legged daughter. We used to like watching some of the cheesy reality TV shows together, like 'America's Top Model', 'Project Runway' and 'MasterChef', and dissecting them, as you do. It's just no fun on your own. You know, it's just sort of … meh. I still dissect them out loud by talking to myself. Yep, now we're back to that old chestnut again.

Scenario Three

The other little challenge for me is the practical side of living on my own. Having had a strong handyman in my life for some years, I didn't have to face this particular challenge. But now, for example, when I want to lift something heavy, I either break my back trying to move it or just have to leave it there.

If you are like me, when you make up your mind you want to move something, and have a slightly fixated, obsessional personality like mine, this will drive you mad. All you can do, ultimately, is glare at said item. There is also the challenge of not being able to open things, like jars or, God forbid, the bottle of wine. You know, that's a crisis situation right there, people!

Scenario Four

I will now share a real-life personal situation I experienced. This is not a made for television moment.

I can't remember what event I was going to, but I was trying on outfits and had put a dress on that I thought would be perfect. As luck would have it (not), the zip at the back of the dress got stuck half-way down and I could not budge it for anything. So, here I was stuck in this dress. It was ridiculously hot, being the middle of summer where I live, so the humidity was about one hundred per cent. And, to top it all off, I was having a menopausal hot flush. Sweat was just pouring off me. I had already spent some time doing my hair and make-up all ready to go out, but I couldn't get that damn zip undone for anything.

Much cursing ensued, while telling the four-legged girls to cover their ears. It took me at least fifteen minutes to finally extract myself from this figure-hugging dress, wriggling out of it, somehow, with my arms stuck above my head. I was absolutely exhausted by the end of it and had to go and have another shower, redo my makeup and choose another outfit before I eventually went out.

That's when the thought came to me, *'What do other people*

do in these situations?' I could have been there undiscovered for days, wrapped up like a mummy. What a horrible thought. Imagine the headline:

*'Middle-aged woman found dead.
Alone for days, unable to self-extricate from a too-tight dress due to dodgy zipper.'*

Not the obituary I've imagined.

Scenario Five-ish — Part A

When my two-legged daughter lived with me, she always sort of—well, you know—if I was going out, she would check and make sure I didn't have anything hanging out that shouldn't be, or tucked in where it shouldn't be, or that I didn't look totally ridiculous as you sometimes worry about when you get over *'a certain age'*. She was someone who gave me the final *'once over'*, so to speak. But as she's not here anymore, it was only a matter of time before something went awry, me being me and all.

One day, I went out to the local supermarket and hardware store as I had some projects I wanted to do over the Easter period. When I got home, I made a phone call to a friend and my earring was knocking against the phone. It was really annoying, so I took that earring out and then I took the other one out. At that moment, I looked down and realised I had gone out with two totally different earrings on. Nothing alike about them at all. One was a stud design and the other a dangling earring. To top it off, I had my hair pulled back in a ponytail. Lordy, people must have thought I was absolutely dotty or that I have early dementia. Maybe I could just say I was starting a new trend?

News flash!!!

The following day I went out, unbeknownst to me, wearing just one earring! No, not trying to revive the eighties. Just totally clueless!

Scenario Five-ish – Part B

Tied in with the clothing and accessory mishaps above was my next, and possibly most humiliating, incident in retrospect. I had an appointment with my solicitor and was running late, so I threw on the easiest dress in my wardrobe. You know, your favourite type—the no-iron, pull over your head, lazy-girl frock that still looks reasonably presentable (well, my favourite anyway). All went well until that night when my two-legged daughter, who was visiting, looked at me, and said, *'Mum, come here.'* I walked over to her, and she said, *'turn around'*.

'Yep,' she said, *'I thought so. Did you know you have a big rip in the back of your dress?'*

OMG, was my first thought. I went to the solicitor's office today, then for a walk down the street to grab a cup of coffee, with a big rip in the back of my dress. People could see my undies! The only saving grace, and it wasn't much I can tell you, was that the dress was navy blue, and I had black knickers on underneath. Imagine if I had worn red, white or flowery patterned undies! It's a precarious ride this living on your own thing, I can tell you!

Scenario Six

My final scenario (for now, anyway—I have an endless supply, but don't want to bore you to death) is the one where I realise having a back-up plan is always essential when living on one's own. I live in a neighbourhood which is great for walking. It has a lovely area with a lake you can walk right around, complete with swans, only a short distance away. As I like to keep my place secure, it is easier for me to exit via the garage and take my garage door remote with me.

On returning from my walk one day, I approached my garage as usual and pushed the remote button to open it and, you guessed it—zip, nada, nothing. That door stayed shut tighter than a toddler's mouth refusing to eat their vegetables. *Great*, I thought, *my two four-legged girls are ensconced inside, along with my keys and mobile phone, and here I am on the other side.*

Trying not to straightaway panic (but who am I kidding, of course I did), I tried to think logically for a solution to this seemingly insurmountable situation. I remembered I had left the back sliding-door unlocked, as the rest of the place was secure and no one could get in. *Hmm,* I thought in all my wisdom, *okay, the logical thing to do would be to try to climb over the front gate and go through that way.*

I could probably refer to myself as a petite person. I am by no means tall and sad to say, pretty unfit and not very flexible. After spending about five minutes trying to scale this quite high gate, looking, I can only imagine, like an uncoordinated mountain goat, throwing my flailing limbs akimbo over it and failing miserably, I realised this was not going to be a viable solution. At this stage. I realised someone may have passed by and seen me and thought:

(a) I was trying to break in
(b) Lord knows—I was too exhausted by that stage to care.

So, obviously, it was time to take a breather and take stock of the situation. At that moment, a light bulb went off, and I thought, *aha! maybe if I open the back of the garage door remote, I can jiggle the batteries and switch them around and that might work.* After about five minutes of trying to open the miniscule battery compartment of said door-opener, while many more curse words were flying around, I finally got it open and success—it worked! After a little air-fist pump, I ran inside to be reunited with my four-legged daughters, who by this stage were wondering what the hell was going on. What a traumatic experience that was! Note to self: *Never* leave the house without a plan B.

So, these are just some of the challenges that can arise on a day-to-day basis in the life of a menopausal, insomniac, crazy dog lady living on her own. I am sure many more will follow. At least I can say my life is rarely boring and I am still learning new stuff, even at this stage of my life. I guess maybe it's all in the way you look at things!

All creatures great and small (OR for the love of God, why?)

It is official. After today's events, I need to live in a bubble or an ivory tower!

I am an animal lover of most types, but when it comes to the rodent variety, snakes, insects such as spiders and roaches and lastly, those disgusting cane toads that have infiltrated our corner of the world, I doth protest.

I'm not sure what God was thinking when he created those *'creatures'*. He must have been having an off day is all I'm saying. If I kept a diary of my *'Encounters of the Creepy Kind',* it would kind of read like this. This first one actually took place a few hours before writing this.

Why? Just Why?

Today I was innocently out in the backyard cleaning up, when I saw something out of the corner of my eye and went to investigate. When I got closer, I saw the hugest, ugliest, cane toad I have ever seen, without a lie. Considering these creatures are meant to be more prevalent in warm weather, after rain and come out at night, clearly this dude had not got the memo. It was winter, hadn't rained in days and it was mid-morning. Shrieking in abject horror, I herded the four-legged daughters back inside to safety and shut the door to protect them and work out my plan of attack.

This is not my first rodeo with these *'bastards'*, as I call them. If I didn't have my girls, I would just shut the door and let them get on with their lives, but they are highly poisonous to pets, and I need to protect the foofy ones at all costs.

There is a lot of advice out of there about how to *'take them out'*, and some of this *'advice'* is as follows:

- There is the *'catch them and put them in the freezer option'*. Apparently, this is the humane way to do it (I don't know, is it humane to kill anything on purpose?). Well, let me just say it straight here, people, and don't worry, I can handle the backlash:
  (a) Hell could freeze over before I bring a cane toad into my house, let alone put it somewhere I store food.
  (b) That would involve picking it up and, let's face it, that's just never going to happen.
- Someone once told me their kids enjoyed getting out a golf club, substituting the golf ball with a cane toad while yelling out *'fore'* (I made that last bit up, I have no idea about golf), sending that critter up into the stratosphere. Clearly that won't work for me as I have no golf clubs and, even though I detest them, just … no.
- My preferred method, as I do have to deal with them somehow and can't pretend I don't, is one that someone shared with me. It is to fill up a spray bottle

with disinfectant and bravely get close enough to spray one said yuck creature. They are meant to hop off and die somewhere, hopefully in the next district.

So, back to today's horrific encounter. Luckily, I had a bottle of disinfectant handy and sprayed enough on it to kill about twenty cane toads, at the same time yelling, '*Die you bastard*!'. However, it took a couple of feeble hops, stopped in the middle of the lawn and looked up at me, as though it was saying, '*So, Einstein, what's your plan now?*'

Drawing on all my basic survival instincts, I scanned my environment and, out of the corner of my eye, spotted an empty plant pot from my recent foray into gardening. I ran over and I put that sucker on top of it, and then a bucket on top of that, and for extra protection, put a few stones on top. Ha, I thought, I can do this solo tough girl stuff after all!

Taking a big breath, thinking this traumatic encounter was over, I took probably less than half a dozen steps when what did I see? Another bloody cane toad, half-hidden in the grass. OMG, is this some kind of conspiracy, or what?! So, rinse and repeat. I now have two buckets on my lawn with captives underneath. I'll be ringing the lovely next-door neighbour shortly to ask

Real-life photo of bucket with captive inside …

him to come and dispose of said items. I do have a line I will not cross ...

You had one job ...

The four-legged daughters have received their first verbal warning for failing to protect me.

They may be my cute love bugs, but when I was sitting watching TV and relaxing the other night, I saw something out of the corner of my eye and watched in abject horror, as a mouse or rodent of some type casually sauntered past me, in no rush, as though it was merely having an afternoon stroll, checking out the neighbourhood.

I squealed, instantly put my feet up and ... crickets. *The girls'* did nothing, just lay tucked up in their beds, probably dreaming of treats. A stern conversation was had the next morning as I handed them their punishment—no treats today. It didn't seem to faze them much that I slept with one eye open all night, wondering if said intruder may venture up the stairs to my bedroom. Off to the hardware store for a mousetrap this morning, but relaxing watching TV is now a thing of the past until this situation is resolved (or I move). Bugger.

Apparently though, a walk-on role was not gratifying enough for the rogue rodent (who I will herein assign the moniker of *'Q'*, because even typing the *'R'* word gives me the heebie-jeebies). He decided that he would like a regular role in my personal soap opera series, *'1,001 Nights at Woody*

Views Way'. Even though he was not booked in, he decided to make a cameo appearance last night once again, as I and the four-legged daughters were fully engaged with the latest episode of *'Canada's Great Bake Off'* (don't judge me).

Again, my acquaintances did nothing, barely a tail wagged as I was screaming and standing on the couch. Q was way too familiar for my liking, seeing we barely know each other, and I swear if he was wearing a hat, he would have tipped it at me before finally making a dramatic exit underneath the door to the garage. In limbo about whether it is worth issuing second warning to furry daughters, as:

(a) They ignored me
(b) I heard rumbles and mutterings between the two of them about going to the *'union'*.

May also take the mousetraps back to the hardware store and ask for my money back!

The start of it all

My love-hate relationship (who am I kidding, purely *'hate'*) with rodents goes back a long way, to when I first moved back to the Gold Coast from Melbourne with my two-legged baby daughter, who was about one year of age at the time. It was just Miss MICDL and me back then. No pets and no partner, as her father had disgraced himself and left the scene (that's a whole 'nother chapter).

I had rented a place that backed onto a plant nursery. I

thought that was a pretty nice idea at the time, until winter rolled around. Apparently, the area I was living in, being near all that greenery, unbeknownst to me in my blissful ignorance, was an appealing holiday destination for field mice in winter.

My shock encounter of the creepy variety played out like this from memory. After a long day at work, and after finally getting my little poppet off to sleep, I was relaxing on the couch watching TV. Against the opposite wall, I had another sofa directly facing me. At one point, for some reason, I felt like someone was watching me. You know when you kind of feel something is wrong and your radar goes off? As I looked over at the couch opposite me, there was a mouse sitting on the headrest, just staring at me with its beady little mouse eyes. I don't know who got more of a fright, me when I saw that mouse, or the mouse when I screamed. I instantly jumped up on the couch as it scampered off somewhere into the shadows.

So, what is one to do when you are living alone and scared to death of rodents? Ring your dad, of course! It must've been a sight. I wish I had could have filmed it. My beautiful dad, who was in his early eighties by then, drove around (luckily at that time my parents were living only about ten minutes away) in his pyjamas and dressing gown, and I remember me being back in my designated position, standing on the couch and him running around with a broom chasing the mouse.

Unfortunately, despite his valiant efforts to catch it and protect me, it was to no avail. He retreated home with said mouse still lurking with intent *'somewhere'* in my house. Well, I instantly knew that no sleep would be had that night. Can a mouse climb up onto a bed? Can it climb up into my little poppet's cot? I would say without a doubt that was one of the longest nights of my life.

In the middle of the night, as I lay there with my ears and eyes wide open, to my absolute horror, I heard scratching sounds coming from the lounge room. (As I am writing this, without a lie, I can feel the hairs on my head standing up on end, even though it was nearly thirty years ago. That is how much it has scarred me.) I got up gingerly, terrified at what I might encounter, and as I neared my stereo (yes, back in the days when we had them), I could hear something in one of the speakers. Primal instinct must have kicked in and like a ninja warrior, I flipped those two speakers over as quick as I could, and quickly ran back into my bedroom after checking in on Baby A.

Dragging myself out of bed the next morning, as I still had to go to work, I drew on all my strength and went over to the stereo speakers. Finding some sort of implement (from memory, I am thinking a spatula, but can't exactly remember because I was so traumatised), I flipped each speaker over and to my surprise and more horror, there was not only one mouse, but two, one under each speaker, dead as anything, stiff as a board, lying there on their backs with their legs up in the air, having suffocated, I suppose.

Poor dad got another phone call and came to take the stereo speaker victims away somewhere. I didn't need to know where. Some things are better left unsaid (and unthought of). Needless to say, when my lease came up shortly after, I did not renew. I'm not a masochist.

We all have our Achilles heel, I suppose, and obviously things that scamper and scratch in the night are mine. Hopefully after writing this tonight, when I go to bed, I won't dream of my encounters of the creepy kind. Luckily, my new digs are not so much of a bubble, but a kind of ivory tower, well up on the first floor with no garden, so hopefully not an appealing holiday destination for creatures of the creepy kind—I hope, anyway!

P.S. Late entry – 'The Wasp Situation'

How could I forget this in the creepy crawly hall of fame! Whilst living on my own, I had a favourite garden swing on the back patio. I used to like to sit on it on the weekends and read a book or just relax. This particular day, I decided to sweep up a bit, as it had been windy the night before and some leaves had blown onto the patio. The swing seemed a bit dusty and cobwebby underneath, too, so in my wisdom, I decided to get the broom and clean it off. Unbeknownst to me, however, a wasp nest had formed. When I valiantly tried to brush off the dirt, I accidentally knocked open a nest full of paper wasps.

Before I could scream, *'For the love of God!'* (sorry again, God!), half a dozen or so wasps decided that my sundress looked like a pretty nice place to hang out and flew up underneath it. In absolute horror, I ran inside and closed the sliding door so hard and fast, I'm surprised it didn't fly off the tracks. I was jumping up and down and screaming, trying to bat these nasty critters out from under my frock as they were stinging me.

The two four-legged girls came to see what the hoo-ha was all about, and thinking I was playing some sort of game, thought they'd jump up on me, as well, for good measure. Somehow, in the midst of all the hysteria, I managed to shoo the offending wasps out from my dress and finished them off with probably nearly a whole can of bug spray. (Again, no judgement please, people. You do what you have to do in these critical situations!)

After a while, when I was sitting down recovering from the trauma whilst applying a washcloth filled with ice cubes to soothe the growing welts on my legs from being stung, I felt a funny little buzzing sensation in the top of my dress. When I peered inside, to my dismay, I saw one sneaky sucker had made its way up into the bodice of my frock and was having a field day. I whacked that thing (and myself in the process) and managed to squash it dead. What the hell! What did I ever do to deserve that!

I also found out in my research afterwards that once you have been stung by this particular breed of wasps, you may actually become allergic to them. Let me assure you right now, I'm not about to confirm that fact. So, I again moved house when my lease was up and from now on, during the wasp-nesting season, I am now like Detective Clouseau whenever I am out in the garden, armed with my can of bug spray and rolled up newspaper!

What cheddars me off (OR enough already)

I'm a pretty positive and happy person, you know, the glass half-full kind, but sometimes, certain things irritate me. I guess I wouldn't be human if they didn't.

One of my all-time favourite TV shows in the past was called *'Hey, Hey it's Saturday'*. For non-Aussies, or people born after my era, it was a variety comedy show with different segments, celebrity guests and acts, never meant to be taken too seriously, which was the joy of it.

One regular segment I always got a laugh out of was called *'What Cheeses Me Off'*. Each week, the host, Darryl, talked about a particular thing or situation that annoyed him. Sometimes, the *'thing'* featured was sent in from a viewer who had written to the show (you know, back in the dark ages when we used to write letters). Usually, they were just simple everyday things most of us could relate to as annoying. We would realise that we humans are all more alike than we thought and all have a good chuckle and a laugh at ourselves.

Lately I realised I have my own list of things that often baffle or annoy the hell out of me, but so as to not infringe on copyright, I have titled my list *'What Cheddars Me Off'*. Maybe you can relate to some of these, too.

Listed in no particular order of priority, they are.

1. Food on top of chips

Now, I don't know who started this trend in restaurants, but they have a lot to answer for. Let me paint the picture for you. You have ordered your chicken parmigiana or steak for example, and, if you are like me, normally go the chips and salad route as opposed to the vegies option. Sitting patiently awaiting your meal, you see the waitress bringing over your plate and—yep, there you go again—the chips are buried underneath the piece of chicken or steak.

I'm not sure what the exact purpose of this arrangement is because we all know that to get to the chips, you are going to have to move said protein off them. Then you've got to rearrange everything on the plate so you can:

    (a) Cut the piece of chicken or steak on a flat surface, not a mountain of chips, to reduce the risk of it flying off the plate.

(b) Get to the chips.

Also, by this time, the once crunchy chips have usually gone soggy from having chosen item on top of them. I just don't see the point in all of it. What *is* its purpose? To make it look like there is more on the plate than there is? Enough already …

Update: I went out for dinner with a dear friend last night and saw this whole exact scenario play out right in front of my very eyes. When her meal of steak and chips was put in front of her, Ms M grumbled, *'I don't know why they put the steak on top—now my chips are all soggy!'* Restaurants, are you listening? Your patrons are revolting!

2. Headache tablets and hangovers

Is it only me or does the headache tablet somehow know when your headache is self-inflicted, so it is totally ineffective in relieving it? This is one of life's mysteries to me and is my own personal truth. I feel nearly like it's laughing at me going, *'Serves you right, Buster—suffer!'* while rubbing its hands together in glee (it's okay, I know they don't actually have hands).

I personally believe there is some sort of conspiracy out there in the pharmaceutical world. In my imagination (unique as it is), I picture a tiny panel of judges sitting at a table holding score cards like the judges do at an ice-skating competition. For example, rating of paracetamol efficacy:

(a) Muscle strain; efficacy of tablet – 8/10
(b) Headache from eye strain; efficacy of tablet – 7.5/10
(c) Headache from self-inflicted hangover; efficacy of tablet – 1/10

3. Opening a tissue box

Now, maybe there is something wrong with me (quite possibly) and I am the only individual who has this issue, but I find it impossible when opening a new box of tissues to extract just one tissue from it. I understand they are trying to give you bang for your buck by smooshing in as many tissues as possible. But they seriously need to redesign these boxes so you don't end up pulling out a big wad of scrunched-up, shredded tissues that usually end up unusable and tossed in the bin. Surely if we can invent things like electric cars and smart watches, someone can figure this debacle out and save me from this situation moving forward.

4. Deodorant marks on black clothing

Again, I don't know if it is just me, but in my fifty-something years, I have never mastered the art of applying deodorant after my shower, then putting on a dark-coloured top or dress without checking out the back of me in the mirror and noticing white marks from my deodorant. I'll think, *surely, I've got it this time. The careful way I wriggled into that, there is no way it could have left a mark.* I'll turn around, contorting myself to look at the back of me in the mirror to check, and … nope, there are those annoying white stripes again! I've even bought the deodorants that claim they, *'Pass the Black T-shirt Test'* and it still happens. Am I doing something wrong? If someone has a method for avoiding this, please share and put me out of my misery.

5. Packaging that you need the jaws of life to open

I'm all for safety, but I think sometimes things have gone too far. I have noticed an increase in items of all types being packaged in that clear, vacuum-sealed packaging that is just about near on impossible to open. Items are encased in thick, rigid plastic with not even a little space to insert a finger, knife or screwdriver to prize it open. And if you can manage to rip it open somehow, you risk being cut by the razor-sharp edges. It's great that it's virtually indestructible, but how the hell are you meant to open it? Again, also frustrating if you live on your own.

I kid you not, I bought a pair of scissors earlier in the year because mine had gone blunt and couldn't get that bloody packet open for the life of me. The irony of needing a pair of scissors to open a packet containing a pair of scissors was not lost on me, don't worry!

6. The fitted sheet

You are probably thinking when I bring this item up, it is because of my absolute inability to refold a fitted sheet how it is supposed to be folded, despite being shown numerous times and watching how-to instructional videos on YouTube. However, the fitted sheet has another challenging aspect to it which … cheddars me off. This could also fall under the auspices of *'Murphy's Law'* (you know, the one where if you drop a piece of buttered bread on the ground, it always lands butter-side down). This Murphy guy has a lot to answer for, just saying!

As I was just putting fresh sheets on my bed five minutes ago, I did the silent 'which is the side, and which is the top' debate? Sizing it up, one way definitely looked like the top. Yep, I was sure of it and *(insert buzzer sound)* no, wrong way, and I had to switch it around again. It's kind of like the vertical or venetian blind dilemma when choosing which cord is for opening and which is for closing. Yep, that gets me every time, too.

Regarding the fitted sheet situation, don't judge me. I was not born with the *'fitted sheet gene'* or the *'parallel parking gene'*, either—whatever …

7. Clothing for short people

Once upon a time, if you were a woman and, say, five foot nine, that was thought of as pretty tall, but not anymore. I know the last few generations of females are taller. It's a fact! All you have to do is look at the teenage girls and young women in your local shopping centre or schools to see there are a lot of tall girls out there. Five foot ten and up is not an uncommon sight. One of my long-time friends, who used to run a shoe store, told me it was rare in our day for females to have a size ten foot, but now it is nothing for them to come in asking for size eleven and up. My darling sister has a theory that it is due to the hormones in chicken and McDonald's. I'm no expert in this field, but there is definitely something going on out there!

Now let me say this up front, I have nothing personally against these girls one bit. I think they are lucky. I always wanted to be taller. Being five foot-ish (it's going down unfortunately, not up), there are certain things you just struggle with. For example, not being able to reach things without someone else doing it for you. Or having to drag a stool to precariously stretch up and grab something off the top shelf, hoping said item doesn't drop on your head. Or climbing on said stool and losing your balance only to fall and break something. This is especially annoying if you live on your own, and you have to wait for someone tall to visit who can assist. One of my biggest bug bears, though, is going to movies and concerts and *always* (stupid Murphy's Law again) being behind a tall person so my view is blocked.

What cheddars me off, in particular, about this changing trend is the length of clothing in shops to accommodate our taller females. Not only do you now have to take up the hem of every pair of jeans or pants you purchase if you are around my height (if there is no 'petite' or 'short length' option in the store, which is a pretty rare occurrence), it applies to just about every clothing item in there. Your pyjama pants, your track pants and dresses. Dresses that may sit just right on a taller girl, drag on the floor when I put them on. I look like a child playing dress-up in her mum's clothing, disappearing under a sea of fabric.

I am, therefore, thinking of starting a support group just for shorter women. We need to band together as we are the forgotten ones. It's discrimination in reverse!

So, these are some of my most cheddarish moments that spring to mind. I'm sure as I continue musing, more will make themselves known to me. I am so grateful that I have been granted the biggest gift in life, and that is the ability to laugh at myself and not take things too seriously. We are all on this crazy rollercoaster ride together, guys, so we might as well have a smile on our faces, joy in our hearts and make it a fun one!

Life begins at forty – Part One: What NOT to Wear

A wise man once told me that once you hit forty your body starts falling apart. Cheery thought, right? I remember thinking at the time, *jeez, this guy is a real barrel of laughs, isn't he?* I was aged thirty-nine at the time and that (wise?) man was the one I had just started dating. He was to become my future husband. I am the annoyingly (probably in his eyes, but then I am just hypothesising) *'glass-half full'* person. You know, the one always wanting to believe the best in everyone and everything. But for the love of God, did he have to be right about this particular philosophy!

He was also the one who shared another snippet of his sage wisdom with me. If you don't get to sleep within the first five minutes of lying down in bed, you will miss the *'sleep window of opportunity'* (when you have read my musings about my sleeping prowess, you will understand this more). Bloody hell. Two bits of his wisdom are dead-set true. Couldn't they be about good things instead of depressing stuff?

Apart from the physical suit I am wearing crumbling in front of my disbelieving eyes, including me seemingly shrinking at an inordinate rate of knots (sorry, I am a being a bit dramatic here, I know), I have also had other experiences making this aging thing apparent, that I am none too pleased about. One of these is my absolute inability to know what to wear anymore. I have cast my mind back to see how this came about, and below I have detailed a chronicle of sorts about my fashion escapades over the decades, to see if I can get to the bottom of this unfolding situation.

I would never say I have been a fashion plate or fashion aficionado during my lifetime, but I guess I cared enough that I looked presentable and didn't stand out for the wrong reasons. My first recall of the importance of appearance would have been due to my dear mother, always an immaculately dressed and groomed woman, having been both an air hostess and a model. As luck would have it for her, I was born into a family who were in the *'rag trade'*. Specifically, my father owned and ran two children's fashion labels, one called *Sweetheart* and the other *Suzie-Q* (I take ownership for the naming of that one).

The sixties

Unfortunately, memories of this time are not my favourite ones of childhood, as my mother had decided in her wisdom to dress my sister and me in identical clothing. Now, I know this can be a *'thing'* when dressing twins, but we weren't twins. As a child, I remember my sister quickly speaking up anytime someone asked if we were twins, which happened on a pretty regular basis because of the dressing identically thing. She would state very clearly, to leave no doubt in anyone's mind, that she was actually two years and ten months older than me.

How times have changed. Now if someone asks us if we are twins, my sister seems to remain steadfastly mute to the question and it is me who quickly pipes up, asserting, *'No, I'm the younger one!'*

Evidence of the 'dressing like twins' phase in identical outfits. I am the one with the cheesy grin on the right …

Clearly not twins

This dressing alike scenario went on for a few years until our voices must have finally been heard. We needed and demanded our own individual identities. Our wardrobe choices were still under the supervision of our mother, though, and I can still recall us wearing a variety of similar looking red tartan frocks, white socks with lacy frills on the top of them and black shiny patent leather shoes for some time after.

The seventies

As a child of the sixties and seventies, my first recall of the *'must-have'* item highly coveted amongst young tweens was a pair of Levi's red label jeans. It couldn't be any other brand. It *'had'* to have that little red label stitched into the back pocket, all of, I would say, three centimetres in length. I think I was about eleven or twelve when I finally convinced my parents that I desperately needed this particular pair of jeans or I would just die (note I was already dramatic back then). I was never a cool kid (still not), and I doubt anyone at that time was checking out the back of me to verify whether I was wearing the original and not a cheap knockoff.

The next particular fashion trend I can recall was also in the early to mid-seventies. At the time, I was a mad fan of an Australian band called Sherbet. As you can probably tell by the name, that was in the time of the so-called *'bubble gum pop'* bands. I cannot perceive a band made up of grown men now ever wanting to be known as Sherbet. Looking back, the seventies was an odd hodgepodge of fashion, but at the time this band dressed in tight satin waistcoats sans shirts, or tight satin shirts left undone to the naval to display their hairy chests, and even tighter satin flares.

I vaguely recall having a pair of satin flares. I can't imagine where I would have worn them to be shown off to the masses, as I was never allowed to go anywhere apart from school, family get-togethers or home. I'm pretty sure they would have been matched with high cork-platform heels at the time, or perhaps the snappy (I thought, anyway) red patent leather *'clogs'* that I clopped about in.

The next *'must have'* fashion accessory on my trip down memory lane was when fake fur zip-up bomber jackets were to die for. Again, it was another *'you can thank the seventies fashion moment'*. My particular jacket of choice was a loud, bright Kermit the Frog green number, proudly worn anywhere and anytime I was able. I cringe at the thought now. It must have looked more like a battered ugly bathmat than a trendy fashion item, definitely a fashion *'don't'* rather than a fashion *'do'*.

Other trends came and went, and like most of us at the time, I embraced the majority of them in my teenage years and young adulthood, wanting to fit in with the crowd as you do at that age. There was the trend of Hawaiian print clothes, either dresses, shirts, boardshorts or a combo of all of them (we lived on the Gold Coast so it was acceptable at the time) along with puka shell necklaces, as worn by David Cassidy and other seventies heartthrobs.

I remember wearing the *'gypsy trend'* in the latter seventies. Elasticised off-the-shoulder tops with layered floral, flouncy skirts and a fake silk flower stuck on a comb, placed in my hair at a jaunty angle. I wore this ensemble to the local nightclub, the Paradise Room (not much Paradise found there, unfortunately, mostly heartache). I do remember feeling very glamourous at the time. Who knows if I looked it though.

One particular trend comes to mind, however, the thought of which I bury my head in my hands and wish the memory would die forever and join my tattered pride. I was about sixteen or seventeen and in my first paid job, when Olivia Newton-John brought out the song, *'Let's Get Physical'*. Yes, I was one of those tragic girls who sometimes wore leg warmers and even a headband around my forehead to work. Although, the closest thing I got to exercise then was walking to the post office and bank at lunchtime. Not much has changed in that regard, either. (Please refer to *Chapter 12 'My chequered history with exercise of the physical kind (or exercise is my kryptonite)'* for further details*)*.

This was at the same time I got my one and only *'poodle perm'*. I swapped my lovely long straight head of hair for a hairdo I could do nothing with, which took years to grow out and looked like a well-used mop perched on the top of my head. I remember coming home from the hairdresser with my new do, and my first boyfriend at the time saying something along the lines of, *'Why on earth did you do that to yourself?'*, which added another hurtful notch to the already growing array on my belt of low self-esteem.

Dear Lord, I managed to dig up the only photo of this tragic hairstyle. I can only imagine I never allowed another one to be taken during this traumatic hair period or burnt any other reminders.

Only existing photographic evidence of poodle perm disaster. Thankfully, it is fuzzy.

The eighties

I remember the eighties as a time that fashion forgot, and for good reason. I think I have blanked out the memory of my wardrobe for most of that decade. I do, however, remember snippets of it, especially in my mid-twenties, when I escaped small-town Gold Coast, Queensland and moved to the big smoke of Melbourne. That was a whole different world then, dressing up to go to work in the city each day.

Of course, it's easiest to recall the music at that time to work out what was in style. I don't remember ever embracing the whole Madonna look. It was a bit too dark and risqué for me. I do remember more business-like clothing and I am sure the odd shoulder pad made an appearance in my wardrobe (think eighties TV show *'Dynasty'*), as well as those ridiculously high-waisted jeans, possibly in an acid-wash, or what we now refer to as *'mum jeans'* … oh Lord.

It was also the era for big hair and a lot of big chunky plastic jewellery. That I can surely tell from going through my polaroids. Who knew hair could be so big? I wish I had had the wisdom to buy shares in a hairspray company back then!

The nineties and onwards

After I had my two-legged daughter in the early nineties, my clothing became less important to me as I focused on her and full-time work. Nothing stands out from this time onwards. I had my work clothes and my weekend ones. I knew what sort of things suited my build and I sort of stuck to that. It was safe. I was comfortable and I didn't feel the need to stand out too much.

But fast forward to my fifties and *woah*! Suddenly, I feel like I am one of those poor women who have been nominated by a *'so-called'* caring friend, relative or workmate for a wardrobe intervention in an episode of *'What Not to Wear'*, being told how dreadfully I am dressing and trying to be rescued from my own bad taste. Everyone seems to have an opinion of what a *'woman of a certain age'* should or should not wear. How come it becomes open slather for people who don't have a stake in it?

I must admit *'What Not to Wear'* was, and still is, one of my favourite shows and guilty pleasures. The hosts, Trinny and Susannah, would pounce unannounced on some poor unsuspecting target, normally in a crowd of people, put them in a dressing room surrounded by mirrors and stripped down to their undies, and tell them what they should and shouldn't wear. As harsh as it sounds, the premise of the show was to actually bolster the target's self-esteem, make them feel better about themselves and was not aimed at shaming them. However, there were the odd one or two over time that refused to give up their well-loved Crocs or tie-dye leggings and you have to respect that.

But never did I think in real life that I would feel as uncomfortable as those chosen ones on the show did. Never did I think it would be *me* in that dressing room. That, it seems, is now where I squarely am.

Is it just us more mature women who people feel they have the right to dictate to about what is or isn't suitable for us to wear? You just have to go online to find a plethora of posts on what you shouldn't be seen dead in once you hit fifty (or even forty) and suggestions of what you should be wearing, most suggestions of which I view as frumpy, vanilla and would surely make us all blend into the background. No thanks, people, I am definitely more a tutti frutti kind of girl!

Why is there no *'What Not to Wear'* show for people *under* a certain age? I doth protest! I see lots of fashion faux pas out and about of all ages, young and old, but would never ever consider walking up to someone and saying, *'I just wanted to let you know that probably isn't the most appropriate thing for you to wear given your age and body shape.'* Just back off, people!

And also, while I am on my soapbox, how come no one gives fashion advice so freely to men as they get older? I am going to write a complaint to someone about that ... just not sure who.

I thought I used to know what suited me and what didn't. Now I question everything. I don't even know what shops to go into anymore. They are either too young or too old for me. I know they are too young for me if I go in and the music is too loud. I know they are too old for me if I go in and see women who would be my mother's age in there. Nothing seems to be in between. Just because I am in my fifties, doesn't mean I want to dress like my nanna. I still want to feel good about myself.

Side note: This last sentence brings back an unsettling memory of being at my local shops last year, wearing what I thought of as one of my favourite tops. It was a paisley one, my favourite pattern, with ties on the sleeves, comfortable (a must have on my checklist) and I thought quite stylish. As I was walking along, I spotted a woman who had to have been in her mid-eighties (from memory, she may even have had a blue rinse through her hair) wearing the same top as me. Aghast with horror, I cast my eyes downwards and quickly made my way back to my car, drove home as fast as I could and put that top in the donate pile before you could say Noni B ... The memory still haunts me today.

As I work from home now, I seem to spend an inordinate amount of time wearing so-called *'active wear'*. As the most active thing I do during a weekday is sometimes venture out to my backyard or the mailbox, perhaps it should be re-labelled *'active wear for people who wish they were active but just aren't'*. I shudder to think I have got to the age where *'comfort'* trumps *'style'*, but it seems that this could be the case.

So, what is suitable for me to wear in society's eyes? Who decides this? Shouldn't it be me? Who cares if I look silly, inappropriate or like mutton dressed up as lamb? Shouldn't all that matters be how I feel about myself? I think I will pitch a show to the networks called *'What to Wear (or Mind Your Own Bloody Business)'*, dedicated to people just like me, which tells us how ridiculously wonderful we are just as we are.

Me, personally, I think I will adopt the outlook of my favourite Aussie icons, Kath and Kim, the queens of self-confidence and *'love myself sick'* … just as I am.

Life begins at forty – Part Two: The wheels on the bus ... fall off

I don't remember being a curious child. You know, one of those kids who always asks *'why?'* to everything they are told, particularly by a parent (possibly also the same kid who always asks *'are we there yet?'* on a family car trip).

Maybe I'm a late bloomer, I don't know, but now I definitely want to know *'why?'* about most things happening to me as I inch ever closer to officially *'past middle-age'* and into the abyss of *'whatever comes after that'* age.

The things I want to know *'why'* about are maybe the things most people also want to know once they hit the golden milestone. So, I have made it my mission in life to document all these pressing issues as they arise and see if I can get an answer from someone, anyone, out there … please?

Issue One: Things falling out

The struggle is *real*, people! It's one of the most distressing situations I have had to face. It's not just men who start to shed their hair as they age, it's women too. Who knew? Whilst it is great not to have to shave legs and armpits as often when this strange phenomenon takes place, it is not so great when it starts to affect visible parts of the body such as my head!

Seeing great swathes of hair on the hairbrush, floor and every possible surface is quite an upsetting experience but apparently it's another cross that Mother Nature in her wisdom has allocated us females to bear (sorry, bit dramatic here, but as I said, distressing situation unfolding). Menopause in all its glory—sheesh! It also drives my slightly OCD husband to distraction. Everything, including freshly washed clothes and towels straight out of the washing machine, has my hair stuck to it.

However, one of the most shocking hair-based experiences for me has been the *'eyebrow situation'*. This actually began for me in my early thirties. One morning, I awoke, looked in the bathroom mirror and thought to myself … *'hmm, that's odd, something doesn't look quite right here.'* Unbeknownst to me, overnight, half of my left eyebrow had turned white. Maybe not an issue if I was blonde, but my hair is dark brown and my eyebrows and eyelashes are black.

I realised later on during my research into this that, due to a particularly stressful and devastating event in my personal life at age thirty, part of my body's reaction when I internalised that stress was to go, *'Okay, something needs to give here. Let's just turn half an eyebrow white. That shouldn't be too much disruption to her life.'*

Well, as a matter of fact, it kind of was. So, after coming to grips with what had transpired, my options were:

(a) Colour my eyebrows in with black pencil.
(b) Dye them.

I didn't even know there was such a thing as eyebrow dye, but I was wrong, and so began my twenty-plus year relationship with this process. Note that this was also before things such as tattooing eyebrows and besides, that would involve needles and pain so … no.

To begin with, if you've never seen yourself or anyone else with eyebrow dye on, I can tell you that the first time can be quite a shock. When I looked in the mirror, I screamed. The first thing that popped into my mind was an image of Faye Dunaway playing Joan Crawford in the movie *'Mommy Dearest*'! Definitely not something you want to do when anyone else is around, or they, too, will run screaming. The first time my four-legged daughters saw me walking around in the midst of waiting for the dye to take, even they were taken aback and looked at me as though asking, *'Who the hell are you and what have you done with that woman who feeds us?'*

After having this done, I feel like I actually have my original face back, which might sound a bit weird, but it is amazing how much eyebrows actually define your face. However, going through this process can still be fraught with its own issues and challenges.

I'm sure my best friend Ms Jo Jo doesn't mind me sharing, we have chatted about how excited we get going to our hairdressing appointment and simultaneously having our eyebrows *'reinstituted'*. The one thing though, is that when freshly done, the eyebrows tend to appear a little more prominent than usual, especially when they are black or dark brown, and are usually the one thing people will notice about you first when they look at you.

As I commented to another dear friend yesterday, after she apologised for her appearance as she had just had her brows *'done'* and they look a little more *'prominent'*, I replied, *'Don't worry I usually say my eyebrows generally enter the room half an hour before I do!'* You just have to just embrace this getting older stuff, don't you think?

Back to the hair loss bit. You know when you stress about things how you tend to dream about them? Well, I do anyway, but then I have always had weird dreams for as long as I can remember. For example, when I was long overdue a checkup at the dentist, as yes, I'm one of those people who do whatever they can to avoid it, I dreamt that all my teeth fell out into my hands one by one. It was horrendous.

This, however, now applies to my hair. I vividly recall one particularly disturbing dream in which I woke up, dragged myself out of bed, looked back and all my hair was still on the pillow. I woke up with my heart pounding and in a sweat. Of course, the first thing I did was raise my head and look at my pillow to double check it was just a dream. Thank the Lord it was!

They say (yes, them again—see reference to *'they'* below) that you lose more hair in summer. So, I guess maybe one of my options is moving somewhere that never has summer, just an eternal winter. Maybe Antarctica? Hmm. Seems a bit drastic even for me.

Issue Two: Sleep

'*They*' say that as you get older, you need less sleep. Who on earth are '*they*'? Whenever I think of this question, I picture a group of old grey-haired men wearing black-rimmed coke-bottle lens glasses, carrying clipboards around and muttering between themselves. Sort of a cross between Albert Einstein and Professor Julius Sumner Miller. (For people not of my era or not Aussie, he was a scientist on TV in the sixties and seventies on a show aimed at children called '*Why Is It So?*', teaching us all about science and such stuff with crazy experiments he would carry out.)

This, however, is a disturbing prospect for me. As mentioned in previous ramblings (or musings), I am an MICDL (Menopausal Insomniac Crazy Dog Lady). I am lucky if I can crack six hours of sleep a night and even that is peppered by frequent waking and much tossing and turning. If '*they*' say I am going to sleep less as I get older, bloody hell … in my calculations, by the time I'm seventy, I'll only be sleeping about ten minutes a night!

As I was lying in bed last night (not sleeping, of course), I was thinking of all the hours of sleep I have missed out on over the years. It's like I am racking up a debt, a kind of '*sleep debt*'. There would be so many zeros on this number, it would be enough for me to open a Swiss bank account. On discussing this with Mr MICDL in the morning, he remarked that if it was a bank account, it would be one I could only deposit in and not make any withdrawals. Yep, that's about the sum of it.

Issue Three: Eyesight

One of the things most of us can't avoid, as the hands of Father Time are whirling around the clock face, is fading vision. You can be in denial as much as you like. People aren't buying it. I know—I have been in denial for over ten years.

How does this affect my day-to-day life? In almost every single aspect. Some of the key points are highlighted below.

1. Putting make up on

It's pretty hard putting eye makeup on when you can't see. Things go awry. I either put on too much or too little and end up looking like a kindergarten student has applied it. I know, you may think just get one of those big magnifying mirrors. I've tried that. I struggle enough looking at myself in a normal mirror, let alone see myself magnified ten times. It's not a pretty sight seeing my pores enlarged that much, or my wrinkles, so I just choose not to put myself through that uncomfortable experience.

It can be dangerous, though, especially handling one of those dreaded mascara wands whilst squinting to see. It can result in either black blobs around the eyes or even the chance of stabbing an eyeball with the end of it. It takes nerves of steel on my part. It's probably why I am choosing to go make up free more often now.

2. Fake eyelashes

Try putting on fake eyelashes instead, you may suggest, in

order to avoid mascara-related injuries. I did try one of those apparently '*foolproof*' magnetic sets that looks so easy in the Facebook ads, but apparently, I am a fool. I tried, and I failed. After half an hour of faffing around with these caterpillar-like lashes with miniscule magnets attached to them, I was so exhausted by the process I just about needed a shower, a Bex and a lie down.

3. Labels

The kitchen is another area that demonstrates loud and clear how much my eyesight has declined. Looking glasses are definitely called for, but I protest loudly to whoever manufactures food labels. Is it really necessary to put so much text on the back of a packet or jar? I suggest using the whole of the label landscape just for the instructions. That's all I need to know. I don't need to know the ingredients. I don't even want recipe suggestions. I purely want to know how to make whatever the product is I have bought.

Some of the writing is so miniscule I can't even read it with my glasses on! I have to use the magnifying app on my phone plus my glasses, to even be able to vaguely decipher the hieroglyphics and, for some inexplicable and cruel reason, the text is usually white, which makes it even harder. Come on, people, a little empathy here for us visually challenged individuals is not asking a lot.

OMG—newsflash! I just had the most amazing idea. What if they had a large print section in the supermarket like they do at the library? Who can I ask about this? Maybe I can patent it!

4. Phone time

Another consequence of failing eyesight is not being able to read my phone clearly. I have had to make the font so big on my phone, I can hardly fit a message on there. I know I am not alone here. Many a time when I am out, I can look around me and see people with that telltale furrowed brow or squinting eyes expression as they are holding their phones out at arm's length, futilely trying to read the screen. Just put your glasses on, people. It's just not worth the pain (or the wrinkles for that matter).

5. Shopping expeditions

I do have glasses. I wear them at home. But when it comes to going out shopping, it's just painful putting them on and taking them off every time I want to look at a price tag. However, after a few embarrassing incidents on my part, I have realised this is not an optional extra anymore.

I confess I have been so loathe to put on my glasses, I have even asked random strangers in the supermarket to read out the use-by date on an item for me. I mutter some excuse like I have left my glasses at home and pick someone who looks kind enough to help me out and believe my made-up story.

I have, on various occasions, taken home clothes that were the wrong size when I haven't felt like trying them on in the store. It is amazing how much a 'five' can look like a 'six', a 'two' can look like a 'three' or even an 'eight'. I kind of got tired of having to return clothes, so decided I finally needed to stop being so stubborn and in denial and actually put my glasses on to read the labels.

However, my biggest and most embarrassing caper was when I was in a store killing time before hopping on a plane to come home after a weekend away. I decided to buy a bra and found one that looked suitable. I couldn't be bothered trying it on, so squinted at the label and thought it looked my size. In my wisdom, however, after previous shopping fails, I decided to double check with the cashier that it was the correct size and she confirmed that it was. At the same time, and in hindsight, she gave me what I thought was a bit of a weird look.

I didn't realise why until I got home and took out said bra. I looked at it *with* **my glasses on** and thought, *what's that funny opening?* On reading the tag, I realised I had purchased a maternity bra. True story. How could I ever make that up? No wonder she gave me an odd look. That definitely taught me a lesson to get over my vanity, laziness and my putting-on-glasses aversion!

6. Dining out

This is another situation I see play out quite often. I know because I do it myself. It doesn't matter how far away you hold a menu with outstretched arms, it doesn't make it easier to read. It's either starve, randomly point at something on the menu when you go up to order or give in and *put your glasses on*! Have a look next time you're out and see if you can pick out the guilty parties. They are out there, believe me.

But, regardless of all the above, I have to admit that at this stage of my life, I think I am more comfortable in my own skin than I ever have been. You just seem to get over yourself and what other people think or don't think about you. I think that is one of the best gifts of getting older.

Whilst the issues I raised are sometimes exasperating to me, just to be here now, enjoying life is much more important than any trivial annoyances. And hey, it gives me something to ponder and write about, so turn that frown upside down. Maybe that decreases the wrinkles, too. One can only hope!

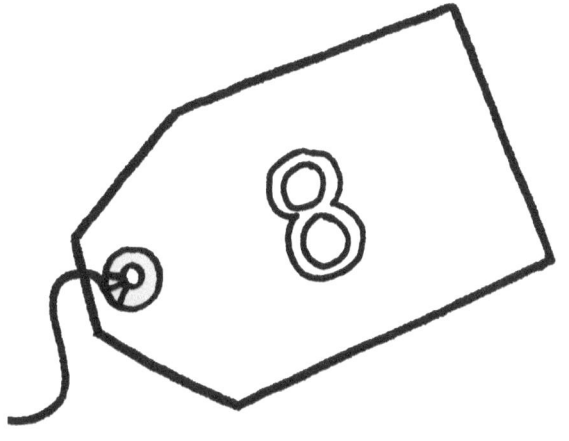

Things my mother told me (OR 'because I said so')

I'm sure it was partly due to the era I arrived in (the 1960s), and the one that my mother was born into (the 1930s), but there sure were an awful lot of mixed messages and advice that my mother fed to me from my formative years onwards that seem to have stuck in my memory.

Whilst at the time some of these statements probably terrified the bejesus out of me as a little girl, it's not until I grew up and tried to make sense out of the myriad of things stated as fact by my mother, that I started seeing the holes in them.

Of course, she ruled the house with an iron fist (actually, it was a wooden spoon), so you didn't argue with or question her, because that would put the spotlight on you—and not in a good way. Therefore, it was best to avoid confrontation and just nod your head in agreement and stop, or in some cases start, whatever it was you were doing at the time this *'advice'* was shared with you.

These are just some of the *'words of wisdom'* still stuck in the memory vault. I am sure there are dozens more:

- *Don't cross your eyes or they will stay that way.*
- *If you stick your finger in the plughole while the bath is*

- *emptying, you will get sucked down the plughole with the water.*
- *If you eat your crusts, your hair will go curly.*
- *If you spill salt, throw it over your left shoulder or something bad might happen.*
- *If your ear goes red and hot, someone is talking about you.*
- *If you swallow the pip in a piece of fruit, you will grow a tree inside you.*
- *Don't tickle a baby's feet or they will stutter when they grow up.*
- *Don't stand behind a lying baby because if you make them look up at you, they will go cross-eyed.*

Then there was the *'advice'* (and I use that term loosely) …
- *Don't sleep with wet hair at night or you will get a cold.*
- *Don't put shoes on the bed or open umbrellas inside because it is bad luck.*
- *Don't laugh at your own jokes as it shows a lack of character.*
- *Don't talk about your achievements or people will think you are conceited.*
- *Don't go swimming straight after you eat, or you will get stomach cramps and drown.*
- *Don't sit too close to the TV set or you will go blind.*

You have to understand that we were the *'seen and not heard'* generation, post-World War II, where the dream family (at least in my household) was a mix between a glamourous

Doris Day movie and living by my mother's *'bible'*, a well-thumbed paperback copy of Dr Benjamin Spock's *'Baby and Child Care'*, which I can clearly remember seeing lying on her bedside table. Let's just say that the *'Doctor'* has a lot to answer for to many adults of my era around the world, but that's another story for another day.

I'm surprised I wasn't terrified for my entire youth of getting struck down by lightning or scarred for the rest of my life if I didn't follow all this sage(?) advice! However, on reflection, I am sure I must have equally bamboozled my own two-legged daughter with my own repertoire of sayings and instructions.

I remember many times, even probably recently, saying to her *'Put something warm on'* and when she replied *'Why?'*, answering *'Because I'm cold'*. Although I am pretty sure that this example is just an innate part of Mumma Bear DNA and one regularly spoken around the world.

Another saying that the poor poppet probably has engrained on her soul is something I unfortunately had to repeatedly say to her when she came home from school in tears, as she was relentlessly bullied throughout her schooling life. *'Be the better person,'* I would say. She will probably get that one put on my gravestone. I'm sure she can reel off a whole swag of the snippets of 'wisdom' (and, again, I use that term loosely) I have given her over the years. I must ask her what they are.

I wonder, sometimes, if being brought up this way at this time in the world brought out the rebel in me. Constantly being told what I could and couldn't do, being watched like a hawk in case something went wrong, was kind of like being wrapped up twenty-four-seven in a bubble wrap of overprotection.

I'm sure, for example, I was the one child, apart from my darling sister, in my whole school who wasn't allowed to learn to ride a bike in case I fell and hurt myself. I wasn't encouraged to do things out of *my mother's comfort zone* like climbing trees, being physical outside and all the fun stuff that kids love, need and should be able to experience. It made me feel like I was missing out on what my friends were doing and it added to my already growing self-view of somehow being *'different'*.

So, maybe once I hit the age of fourteen, my inner spirit that had been pushed down for so long rebelled. I wanted to truly live life and experience it. I wanted to be able to make decisions for myself and make my own mistakes. Of course, this uprising of the true me, and my mother's loosening grip on me, caused much tension and fighting in the household. My poor darling dad was stuck in the middle of it all.

I wanted to quit school and get a job. I wanted my independence and, most of all, I wanted to feel free. So, what did that young girl do? She quit school, got a job and moved out of home at the tender age of sixteen years of age so she could experience life. It was scary. It was exhilarating. There were many mistakes in judgement, things she wishes she didn't do and, maybe, things she wishes she could go back and redo. Somehow, she developed into a pretty okay person, I think. She widened her horizons and view of the world, and, of course, produced the most amazing daughter herself (not sure what this referring to myself in the third person is all about, sorry!).

It's taken fifty-something years, a lot of heartache and tears, as well as the loss of my mother, to reflect on this, to understand, to come to terms with it all finally and know it's okay. I can now look back at this time in my life and see that my mother did everything she did out of love for me and because that's what she equated with love. I now feel finally free to love her for that.

You can only base *'love'* on how it was given to you. We carry this tradition down throughout the ages until we know better and realise sometimes there are much more joy-filled and healthier ways of showing it that will be hopefully passed down to my future (please, God, fingers crossed) grandchildren.

Below is a real actual photo of my sister and me with my mother, me being the pixie looking dot on the right with the dimples.

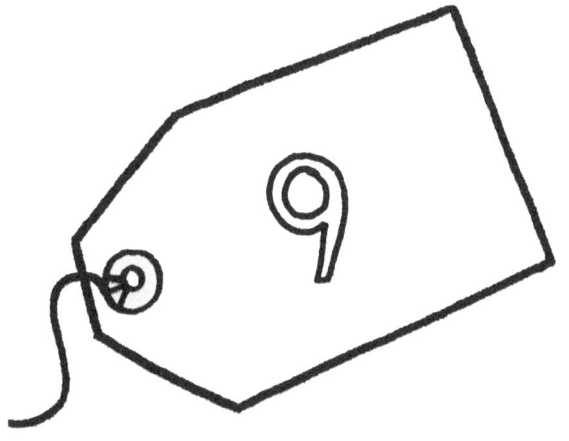

The undomestic goddess

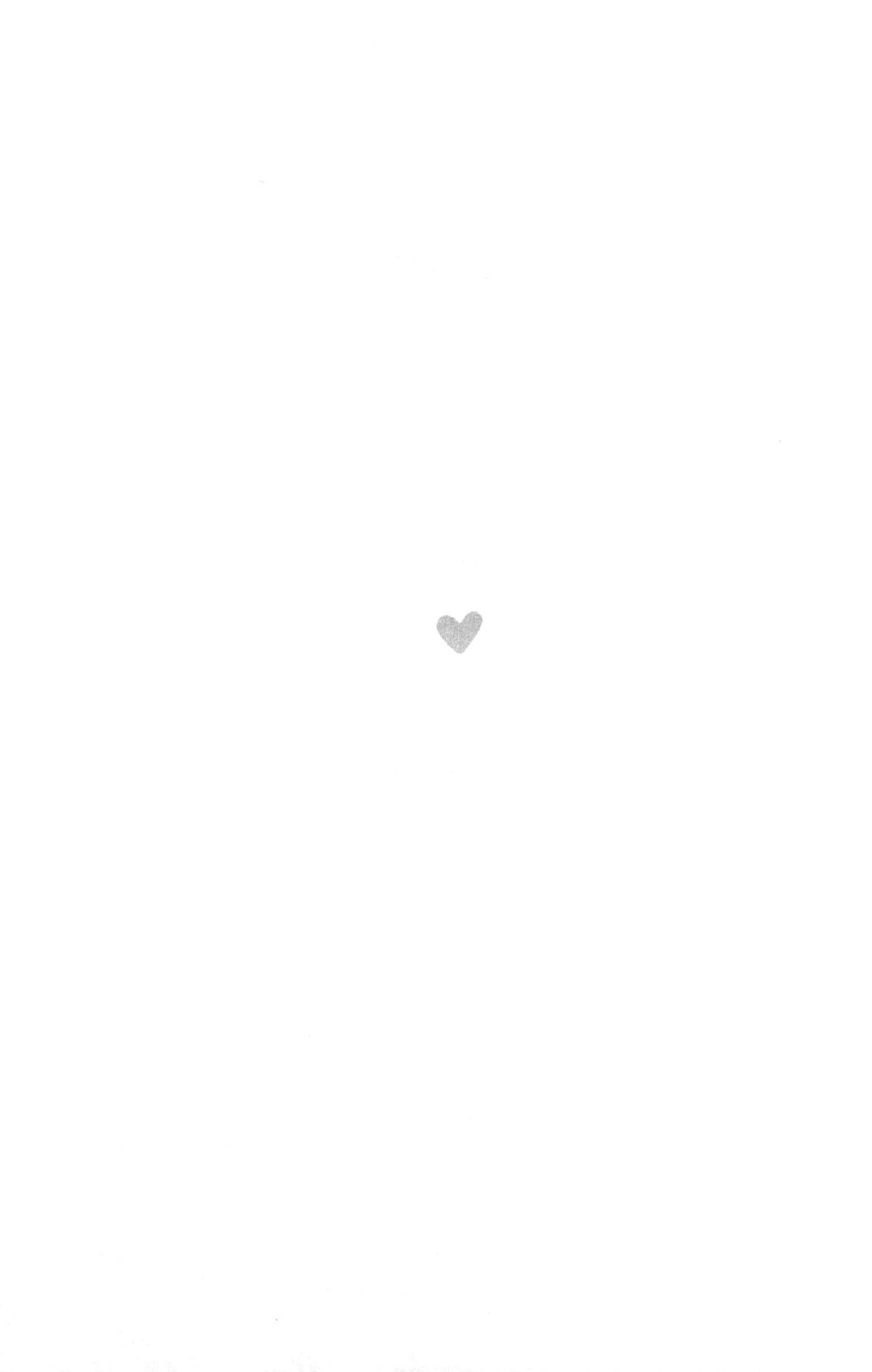

Because I am a member of the female race, I guess some people assume I should enjoy cooking, right? I mean that is my birthright, isn't it? My perceived destiny, part of the mantle I wear, being born one of *the fairer sex*? Well, not so much for me, I'm afraid. I must have been absent the day they were handing out that particular skillset. It is simply not part of my makeup, no matter how much I try to prove it to the contrary, even after all these years.

Thinking back to my childhood, growing up in the 1960s 1970s, I guess it was kind of a foregone conclusion that I would be a pretty basic and ordinary cook. My mother hated cooking and shared this fact with us on an almost daily basis. Her mother hadn't taught her to cook, or perhaps she just had no interest in learning, I'm not sure. Hence, part of the relationship between mother and daughters did not involve us being in the kitchen together, with her sharing her favourite recipes with my sister and I. It just didn't happen.

On the contrary, my memories of childhood meals were ones of pretty much the same dishes on the same nights of the week around the kitchen table. This was topped off with fish and chips from the fish and chip shop most Friday nights (Mum being a lapsed Catholic) and hot dogs or pies on Saturdays when Dad watched the football.

Straining my mind all the way back (it's a bit of a stretch), maybe I have blocked some of those stock standard meals out, or maybe they just weren't that memorable. I remember spaghetti served with meat sauce out of a tin, tuna mornay made from a packet mix, the very occasional lamb roast, and something I think was vaguely referred to by Mum as '*sukiyaki*', a dish that seemed to gain popularity in the late sixties and early seventies—Mum's version, anyway. There was always the obligatory plate of bread and butter on the table, and dinner was usually topped off with some sort of dessert out of the freezer section of the supermarket.

On birthdays, we got to choose our favourite meal. My choice was usually another 1960s classic called '*Chicken a la King*', a creamy chicken dish made with a can of cream of chicken soup, with a dollop of frozen mixed vegies thrown in for good measure, served with rice.

Now and then, however, Mum read something in a magazine about nutrition and would decide that, as a responsible mother, it was imperative our household follows suit. It will forever be burnt into my memory, the evening she decided that my sister and I needed to eat *'lambs' brains'*, perhaps to enhance our own growing grey matter, who knows! There was no disguising what it was though, and as Mum was no Julia Childs in the kitchen, it was somehow cooked, most likely boiled, and dumped unceremoniously on a plate in front of us.

We were also the generation where you were expected to eat whatever was served to you, regardless of what it was, and to finish everything on your plate. However, on this occasion, you couldn't get my darling sister and me to put a forkful of that monstrosity near our mouths without gagging. No way, José. Hell could freeze over first!

Interestingly, however, my mother chose not to partake in this particular experimental dish and took herself off to bed, leaving my poor darling dad to sit there with us until we finished it. Before she flounced off and took her leave to bed, we were told we could *'sit there till midnight'* until we did. (You've got to love the crazy things that come out of parents' mouths).

I can't remember exactly how Dad disposed of the *'evidence'* to this day, but I know that, even though we went to bed slightly later than usual, we were somehow saved from the dreadful fate of consuming any of that God awful dish. Thank you, Dad!

Then there were the occasions where Mum hosted a *'dinner party'*. Whenever visitors came over, Mum had a couple of well-rehearsed meals up her sleeve. However, she usually stressed for the week before to ensure everything was *'perfect'* in her eyes. She'd set up the formal dining room with the good silver and tableware, and like the good little girls that we were, we sat quietly and watched the evening's proceedings unfold.

It also usually took Mum a few days to recover from these events with the stress she heaped on herself. Thankfully, these occasions were few and far between.

Mum also did try to cook some of the dishes from my father's heritage, him being of Lebanese descent. I remember her spending hours in the kitchen on special occasions, assembling a big pot of cabbage rolls or vine leaves and other family recipes that my nanna had shared with her. God bless her, she did try. I'll definitely give her that.

However, absolutely no baking took place growing up in our household. I know that with certainty. The only thing I would classify as *'baking'* was something out of a packet, perhaps for a school fete or the like, where all the mums were expected to contribute something to the cause. For my mother, this usually consisted of a packet of White Wings fairy cake mix from memory, something that I can only aspire to, being the non-domestic goddess that I am.

I'm not saying I was deprived in any way when it came to food and eating. Not at all. Quite the opposite, actually. Memories of my childhood include much eating out at restaurants, usually on a weekly basis, if not more than once a week. This was probably a pretty unusual situation for most kids growing up in the sixties and seventies, but for us it was normal. My dad was an understanding and kind man, and I guess he needed to eat, too!

My parents had their favourite restaurants that we frequented. As a result, we were privileged to be educated in different types of cuisine. I have memories of restaurants such as the Barbecue Inn or Jimmy's Chinese Restaurant where we sat while Mum and Dad consumed a bottle of wine between them, usually a Coonawarra claret or a Mateus Rose. Sometimes they even polished off a liqueur with their dessert (no worries about drink-driving back in those days!). Again, most times, like the well-behaved little girls we were, my sister and I would fall asleep at the table while we waited for them to finish.

As a result of all of this, when I left home in my teens, I had no idea how to cook anything apart from toast. Seriously, I didn't even know how to boil an egg. It didn't seem to matter much at that stage as I tended to eat out a lot socially or just have takeaway.

When I met and moved in with my first serious boyfriend, he knew how to cook and that is, I guess, where I learnt my first few basics such as meat and three vegies, as well Apricot Chicken served with mashed potato (another seventies classic). Unfortunately, my cooking prowess never seemed to develop much past that. It kind of stayed, how should I put it … static.

I was never interested in pouring over cookbooks, testing out new recipes or just winging it and throwing things together from the pantry to create a dish. I guess working full time from the age of sixteen until now, raising a child on my own and coming home after a long day at work, the last thing I would get excited about was what culinary delight I was going to whip up that evening. However, like my darling Mother, I did, and still do, try. I'm just not that good at it!

I don't know what it is about me—I think I'm a pretty intelligent person—but when it comes to following a recipe, it seems the messages misfire on the way from my eyes to my brain. I think have a disorder. I call it the *'misreading recipe disorder'*.

It shows up in two main ways:
Number One: leaving ingredients out.
Number Two: leaving recipe steps out.

These perhaps contribute towards my reticence in trying out new recipes. I feel I have set myself up for failure over the years with this *'disorder'*. It's become a running joke in our family.

I also have an aversion to anything to do with baking. I can make a packet cake fail. No exaggeration. Ask my daughter. She will be delighted to let you know it is true. The thought of attempting anything with pastry makes the hairs on the back of my neck stand up. I'm not even talking about making pastry from scratch. I'm talking about the stuff that just comes in packets ready-made. It's like my arch nemesis (similar to my one with exercise and sweating—see *Chapter 12*).

OMG—hold the press! I don't believe it—I've been pipped

at the post. I just looked up Mr Google and there *is* an actual disorder associated with cooking!

'*Mageirocophobia* is the irrational fear of cooking.'

I'm going to self-diagnose myself with that. Finally, a name to put to what I've got!

It seems kind of silly to let something like this get the better of me, but I have come to the realisation, after all these years, that it is simply the truth and something that I have to accept about myself. That doesn't mean I don't enjoy eating baked goods and I am an avid fan of '*The Great [insert country name] Bake Off*' and '*MasterChef*' and watching others master their art. It just means it is never going to happen for me in this lifetime, and I have come to peace with this fact.

I do exaggerate a little about my own cooking prowess. I can actually throw together a few decent meals and haven't given anyone food poisoning yet (as far as I know). I just get stressed about trying new recipes and failing, as silly as it sounds. I have become a master at doing quick and easy tasty meals with minimal ingredients and as few steps as possible. I share those with my best friend, and we laughingly decided I could compose a cookbook called something along the lines of '*Quick & Easy Tasty Meals for Women Who Like to Drink Wine*'. (I haven't copyrighted this idea either yet).

The interesting thing is I think I have come full circle and turned into my mother. Now it is me who seemingly cooks the same set of meals each few weeks, rotating the dishes around, and stresses whenever any guests are coming over. Luckily, I have a partner who doesn't care what I put in front of him on the table. He is just grateful that I cook anything at all!

All those years of saying silently I don't want to be anything like my mother, oh, the irony of it. Some things are just destiny, aren't they? Isn't it funny what the Universe has in store for us, probably with a huge smile on its face as it watches on. Buon appetito!

Is it just me or ...?

Sometimes I wonder if my brain works differently from the average human. Or maybe I just have a different perspective on the way I view and experience the world around me compared to others. Not saying that's a bad thing. I guess I've noticed it a lot more while living on my own.

I feel like the older I get on the outside (the physical bit), the younger I am becoming inside. It's as if I'm observing and experiencing things with more childlike wonder, innocence and play. Maybe all that time and money spent on endless self-development and spiritual shopping (or *'navel gazing'* as a wise woman I know once coined it) is finally starting to pay off!

I have to say that as uncomfortable as life has been through this process (and believe me, holding a mirror up to yourself and your beliefs can be pretty bloody uncomfortable), maybe this is what I have been unconsciously searching for all along. The opportunity to truly enjoy the lighter side of life, without needing or wanting something back in return. To laugh at myself, not taking everything so seriously or trying to manipulate things in order to get the results I *'think'* I want.

So, if you are ready for it (or not, that's okay, you can stop reading here no offence taken, I'm not for everyone), this is an insight into some of the thoughts that this menopausal, insomniac, crazy dog lady has as she goes through her day-to-day life.

Thought One

When I purchased a property a few years ago, I knew it was the right one the moment I laid eyes on it. I could feel and see myself living in it. Now, most people would be looking around trying to picture how their furniture would fit in and the like. Not me. My first thought was, *'Where will I put the Christmas tree?'* (Christmas is my *favourite* time of year. I would have the tree and lights up all year round if I could!) Luckily, I could see the perfect spot for it, which just confirmed its rightness.

Thought Two

I have a doona cover set in one of my favourite colours—purple. It's the sort of purple they may have named Cadbury chocolate purple. You probably know the one I mean. This doona set has gold love hearts on it. Each pillow has a big love heart on it where I lay my head at night. As I was making my bed one morning, I was quite disturbed to notice that I had put the pillow the wrong way around, with the heart pointing down instead of up. The first thought that popped into my head was, *'Oh no, all the love will drain out!'* and I quickly rushed over to rectify the situation and turned it right side up. Phew, that was a close call!

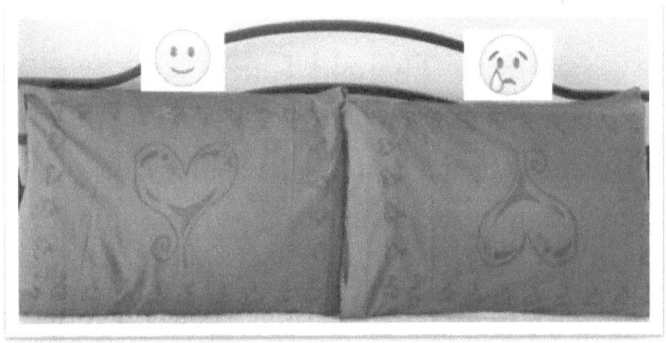

Actual real-life action shot of my pillows, demonstrating said unfortunate 'pillow gate' incident.

Thought Three

As mentioned, my mind seems to be wired differently from other people. Just ask Mr MCIDL—he will confirm this. The other day, when I was drying my crockery and putting it away, a random thought popped into my head. We only ever use the top four or so dishes in a stack of eight. I never rotate the crockery. So, the crockery down the bottom never gets used unless we have a rare dinner party.

This made me think. Is that crockery wondering what its purpose is if it doesn't ever get used? Does it feel like it is missing out, being stuck in the cupboard in the dark, instead of seeing the light of day like its buddies? Kind of like FOMO (*fear of missing out*) for plates and bowls? When this thought sank in, I made it my mission to rotate them at least once a month, so they get the chance to see the light of day with the others ... because I care.

Thought Four

With the encouragement of my BFF, I have discovered the joy of pottering in the garden and growing things in pots (and lots of trips to my new favourite place Bunnings!). Referring back to an earlier musing where I was lamenting on short-girl problems, this can be an issue with hanging pots. I need to precariously stand on a chair in order to water them. One day, I took them down to give them a decent water and some sunshine and was horrified to see that some of the flowers had died. I was devastated. As I removed them from the pot, I apologised to them. It was a sombre moment. Even the four-legged daughters stopped and looked on in horror. I murdered plants. I am a plant murderer. The shame and guilt made me promise the other plants that it will never happen to them—a solemn plant promise.

Thought Five

Have you ever woken up in the middle of the night knowing you need to get up and go to the bathroom, but if you do that:

(a) you will get cold.

(b) you will wake yourself up so much that you can't get back to sleep.

I had this happen to me the other night when I was staying at my best friend's place.

It's like this constant arguing with myself in my head. It kind of goes something like this:

Sensible me: *'Just get up and get it over with. You know you won't sleep well if you don't.'*

Rebel me: *'But it's too cold and dark and I might walk into a wall or trip over the cat.'*

This can go on for most of the night, which kind of defeats the whole purpose, because you don't end up sleeping anyway and chastise yourself for not getting up.

By the way, when I first met my partner, if one of us got up in the middle night to go to the bathroom we would often say to the other, *'Can you go for me too?'* P.S. It didn't work …

Thought Six

Going through my belongings recently, I came across an assortment of odd things that, for some reason, I've felt compelled to keep. I'm not sure why. I hadn't really contemplated them before. I found a plastic bag stuffed with those little twisty tie things that come off the cords of electrical goods and the like. You never know when those things might come in handy, and you know Murphy's Law (this Murphy person has an awful lot to answer for!). If I throw them out, I will definitely need one at some point and will kick myself for throwing them out.

I also found a box in my bathroom drawer crammed full of the extra buttons in the little plastic packets that come with clothing that has buttons on them. I again felt compelled to keep them, even though I have to say on reflection I have never, ever had to use one. But you just never know!

The other thing I have hoarded for many years are those little bottles of shampoo and conditioner that you get in hotels. Just in case I go away, I can take them with me to save taking a big bottle. Considering I rarely go anywhere anymore (regardless of what is currently going on in the world), it may seem odd to some that I collect them.

Miss MICDL often says, *'Mum, I don't know what you hold on to that stuff for'*, but a while back, when she came to stay, she ended up needing to use one to wash her hair, which confirmed my conviction for doing this. *'See,'* I proudly told her, *'I knew someday these would come in handy!'* (However, I did acquiesce somewhat when sorting and threw out the multiple packets of hotel shower caps and shoe-polishing cloths).

Thought Seven

For the last twenty-plus years, whenever I move, I've been carrying around with me a big plastic tub filled to the brim with Miss MICDL's various Barbie dolls and accessories. You know, you've got your Barbie VW Bug, camper van, ballet studio, Barbie clothes, shoes, jewellery, dinner set, etc., and many Barbies in different states of dress or undress. Blonde Barbie, brunette Barbie, redhead Barbie, Barbie's little sister Kelly and, of course, one can't forget Ken. You name it, we've got it. Barbie has got a pretty good life, by the way, I must say!

However, my daughter is not interested in keeping them. This obsession is mine alone. Why might you ask? For the potential granddaughter I don't have yet, of course! Now, you might think, how does she know she will have a granddaughter and not a grandson? Because I just know, that's why.

Nonetheless, looking back to when my one and only child was born, I was absolutely certain that she was a he. It wasn't until the doctor said, *'it's a girl'*, that I realised my intuition was way off on that one. As my mother said to me at the time, *'God gives you what you need'*, and I thank Him or Her every day that they decided to give me my precious daughter.

I was so certain I was having a boy that I hadn't even picked out a girl's name. Thankfully, I had a unisex one in mind for the son I never had, so that was lucky. The backstory behind the name Alex (my daughter groans when I share this story with anyone) was that my favourite show at the time was

Family Ties. I adored the character Alex P Keaton, played by Michael J Fox, so Alex it was.

Thought Eight — Is there a word for that?

I have certain words and phrases that I like to use because saying them just makes me feel … well, happy!
Some of these are, in no particular order:
- *Sassy*—I said this so much, my two-legged daughter bought me a T-shirt. However, I haven't had the nerve to wear it in public—more of a wear-around-the-house item.
- *For the love of God!* (sorry, God)
- *Twee*—just love the sound of that word but had to look it up as I didn't know what it meant. So, here you go, according to Mr Google: t/wi – *adj. excessively or affectedly quaint, pretty, or sentimental.*
- *Juxtaposition*
- *Serendipity*
- *Sassafras*

I find living in this state of being so much lighter, fun-filled and joyous. If I could bottle it up and give it away, I would. Sure, life has its challenges and, like me, many others have experienced them, but as the old saying goes, '*When life gives you lemons, make lemonade*' and instantly you can feel the shift.

The rhythm of the night (at 14 Woody Views Way)

A s I lie in bed with eyes wide open, I feel the rhythm of the night playing out, like a musical score from some obscure Off-Off-Broadway musical. Mr MICDL is playing his allocated part in the orchestra, and me, mine.

I have mentioned previously that I am a very light sleeper. When I met Mr MICDL in my late thirties, he was my soulmate in more ways than one. He was also missing the *'good night sleep gene'*, but times ten.

Upon starting our relationship and having sleepovers, even I, who I thought of as a seasoned professional of the sleepless-night ensemble, was put to shame by this highly acclaimed master of his craft. He won, hands down, no contest. I was amazed at how many things could affect the balance of his sleeping act. It made my simple tossing, turning and lying there staring at the ceiling seem amateur in comparison.

It brought into play things that drove him mad, such as a crease in the bedding underneath him, uncomfortable clothing, clothing that was too tight or rode up, blankets that were too hot or heavy, pillows too soft, the sound of the motorway in the far distance, ticking clocks. It was obvious to me from the start that I was out of my league. We often joke about how we need to sleep in a temperature-controlled bubble, sound proofed, too—that goes without saying.

He, however, has also brought something to the fore that I have not experienced for many a year ... a grown man snoring. Not only snoring, but full-on sleep apnoea. No doing things by halves for this dynamic duo! Now in my late fifties, add menopause into our arrangement and the end result is, well, less than optimal.

This is kind of how the *'musical score'* unfolds ...

Act One: The race to the starting line

Honing our own individual techniques, we begin the race to who can fall asleep first. This is an important advantage to secure at the beginning of the night and a prize held tightly onto. I am usually, alas, not the victor in this particular race. Another run on the scoreboard for Mr MICDL, but, as I said earlier, he is a master in his own right and I bow to his skill. Having failed this crucial starting block, I am already behind in the race to the finish of our evening concerto.

Act Two: The midnight serenade

This act is all about the different pitches and chords of the snore sonata. Who knew there were so many variations? For simplicity's sake, I have given each their own individual title.

1. The 'pfffttt'

This is the less innocuous of them, but don't be fooled by its gentle cadence and sound. It hides a secret crescendo all of its own. It usually begins after Mr MICDL has first drifted off into sleep. A little *pfffttt* sound escapes from his pursed lips. It sometimes brings a smile to my face just hearing it. However, don't be fooled. It has a hidden, darker side because after a while a huge *pfffttt* is expelled, having built up over the ticking minutes. Not so pleasant when lying facing one other and the *pfffttt* is felt abruptly on my bare face, complete with sleep breath. This calls for my *'rollover'* manoeuvre, complete with bed bounce for dramatic effect.

2. The 'nose whistle'

Not always a regular contributor, this part played by the wind section of the orchestra makes special guest appearances on occasions.

3. The 'snort'

This sound effect usually eventuates after the *pfffttt*, most normally experienced when Mr MICDL is lying on his back and has fallen into a deeper level of slumber. It is usually loud enough to make both of us jump in fright (and possibly the neighbours who share the bedroom wall with us, as well as the four-legged foofy ones lying outside the door). It could result in another rollover manoeuvre from me or, if particularly cranky and sleep starved, even my own exclamation or sound of some sort.

4. The 'full blown snore'

The final and most spectacular of all in the snore sonata is the *full blown snore*. This is also when the *'Rule of Three'* usually comes into play (see below, under *'The Disappearing Act'*). As I said, this man is a master in his own right and his reputation precedes him. Even my two-legged daughter (who also had her own sleep challenges and snore-fest sonata in play with her partner) commented that she could hear Mr MICDL through the closed bedroom door and down the hallway, such is the extent of his mastery and talent.

Thank God I love him, is all I can say. The poor man is exhausted, and this is why the *'Rule of Three'* and the blessing of the spare room were created. We all need our sleep, and if that is the only way he can achieve it, then I need to respect that. However, in all fairness, there have been times just before I retreat to the spare room, where I confess, I have uttered in exasperation *'for the love of God!'* (sorry again, God) and thought about employing the use of a peg on his nose.

Act Three: It's getting hot in here

When we first met, Mr MICDL introduced me to something that changed my sleep forever, the latex pillow. After years of sleeping on top of two ordinary pillows, usually waking with a crick in my neck, this was a hallelujah moment for me, and I have never gone back.

After decades of heavy manual work and wearing out

nearly every joint in his poor body, Mr MICDL finally purchased a special bed where the mattress is split in two and controlled by a motor which can go up and down at either end, supposedly to get into a comfortable position. It's kind of like sleeping in a big warm hug, although one has to be careful not to roll too close to the centre (what I personally have named *the vortex*) or there is the risk of getting sucked into the gap between the two mattresses.

However, the main drawback from this luxury sleeping option is that it is made of latex. That stuff heats up quicker than you can say *'self-combustion'* and takes forever to cool down. I may have mentioned that we live in a tropical climate where winter goes for, oh, I don't know, probably about three weeks. Couple that with a latex pillow, and our cosy love nest quickly turns into more of a Swedish sauna.

Also, in order to stifle the sounds of snores, I often need to sleep with a pillow over my head in a vain attempt to drown them out—not the most effective of strategies, but desperate times call for desperate measures. So, after our bed and pillows reach maximum temperature, a random arm or leg may be desperately thrust out of the covers, or the covers hastily thrown off altogether, and the need to resort to sleeping on top of them may also be called for. As a menopausal, insomniac, crazy dog lady, I don't need any additional help to make me self-combust. I've got that one covered all on my own, thank you very much. This is also when the *'Disappearing Act'* (see below) may be used.

The disappearing act

This is an optional act and a part that can be played by either myself or Mr MICDL. For Mr MICDL, this role is seized upon when, after sleep failing to make its presence known, he can no longer endure the heat of the bed or finds it impossible to get into a comfortable position. In desperate need for rest and to protect me from much thrashing and turning, he makes a hasty retreat to the *'spare room'*.

For myself, I usually choose the disappearing act when I realise I have not slept a single wink and the *'Rule of Three'* has come into play. The *'Rule of Three'* is a highly complex (not really) tactic developed by me (and perhaps others who sleep with a partner who snores). This entails three attempts at gently disrupting the snore sonata, usually by a light brush of the shoulder, arm or back or a minuscule tap to some area of the upper body—kicking, violent shaking or similar harsh actions are banned from this tactic. That would be mean, and I'm not mean. This normally results in Mr MICDL turning over or changing positions and interrupting said snore recital.

However, there is a limit for this tactic and after three attempts, if said snoring resumes and the *'Rule of Three'* has failed, then the *'Disappearing Act'* is played and off to the spare room I go. But do not think of the *'Disappearing Act'* as a solution to all our sleep challenges. This, too, has its pitfalls …

However, in the spirit of fairness and transparency, it's unkind of me to simply reflect on Mr MICDL's part in this evening sonata without revealing my own contribution. As mentioned in an earlier musing, during sleep time, I engage in what is known amongst many menopausal women as the *'rotisserie chicken'* manoeuvre. This consists of much rolling from side to side in an attempt to get comfortable and to douse the self-combustion feelings alluded to previously.

I have also been known to mutter and call out in my sleep like some crazy person, and throw my arms and legs akimbo whilst fighting off unknown assailants in my dreams. I have at times been roused by a gentle shake or touch by Mr MICDL, kindly trying to wake me from whatever nightmare I am experiencing. Coincidentally, this can occur at the exact moment he has fallen into or been enjoying a peaceful slumber of his own. I accept my role in this wholeheartedly and unashamedly.

The finale

Bleary-eyed, we each arise the next morning after our individual roles are completed, ready to face the day (sort of and with much caffeine imbibed), only to regroup again that evening and once again play our respective parts.

On reflecting about this whole sleep *'situation'*, the lyrics of an old song played over and over in my mind … *'Till I'm six feet under … live while I'm alive … sleep when …'*

Yeah, right, Mr Bon Jovi. Clearly, whoever penned that flippant line isn't missing the *'good night sleep gene'* and has never had a bad night's sleep in their life, so they don't know what they're talking about! *Sweet dreams x*

My chequered history with exercise of the physical kind (OR exercise is my kryptonite)

My thinking mind (the somewhat intelligent part of it) knows that my body needs exercise to live as long and healthy a life as possible, but the rest of my mind just rebels. Sort of an *'aversion-to-exercise disorder'* (I think I've come up with another *'thing'*).

So, where has this aversion come from, you might wonder (or not, and that's okay)?

To be honest, I was never a *'sporty'* or well-co-ordinated kid, quite the polar opposite. I envied those girls at my school who were, you know, good at everything they tried. I vaguely remember having tennis lessons before school, which from memory I don't think I minded too much, but I certainly was never going to be head-hunted for Wimbledon by any stretch of the imagination.

I also didn't like sports where I could be injured, which probably hails back to being a *'wrapped in bubble wrap'* child. I was terrified of hockey and the sound of those hockey sticks clacking against one another, the hockey ball or perhaps a stray leg that got in the way. I was also afraid of being hit by a softball—or any sort of ball used in sports class, for that matter.

My absolute worst nightmare, though, was when the

hurdles were put out or worse—ugh, high jump. These legs were not made for leaping anything, nada, zip. Definitely worth bunging on a mystery illness and getting sent to the sick bay for, if at all possible.

I was also the kid (there is always one), who was one of the last to be picked for a team on sports day. Usually, me and a couple of the other not-cool or sport-deficient girls were left standing when the teams were being decided by the team captain. Let's face it, I don't blame them, especially when they are competitive. But boy, you don't forget how it made you feel as a kid. I would much rather have hung out at the library than have to go through that embarrassment one more time.

We also had compulsory ballet classes, which I remember as a form of torture for uncoordinated little Suzie. The ballet teacher Miss R—a former professional ballerina—was a bit of a tyrant. She walked with her feet permanently turned out, or in ballet terms, *'First Position'*. She also wore a whistle on a rope around her neck. When it became too much for her to cope with a room full of little girls in leotards chattering, whilst attempting pliés or twirling around the room, she blew on that thing like she was a drill sergeant in the army and we all had to jump to attention.

I dreaded the end-of-year

Note the teacher displaying 'First Position'

ballet concert and hoped and prayed I either got sick and couldn't participate, or that I was placed in the back row up on the stage. They usually held it in a town hall somewhere and there was always lots of excitement about putting on tutus and accessories (for some kids, not me).

I remember the time the end-of-year concert was held at the Dallas Brooks Hall in Melbourne. (Apparently, it was demolished in 2015, along with my harrowing memories.) We were supposed to be dressed as angels on this occasion, wearing handmade halos, made out of wire and silver tinsel by a parent, and holding little torches. We didn't have our own individual halos. We just grabbed what was there out of a community box.

As I hated pushing, because I liked my personal space—and still do—I was the last to grab my halo. Well, whatever *'crafty'* parent made mine, obviously had no idea about what size a six- or seven-year-old girl's head was and clearly made it to fit a head the size of a doll. The memory of running onto stage (thank God I was in the back row), trying to hold on to a halo that was too small for my head and holding a torch that didn't work, let alone attempting any dance moves, still haunts me to this day.

Some teachers and parents have no idea the trauma they put children through when it comes to creative expression through dance—especially if they have no talent.

As an adult, I have one overriding reason for my aversion to exercise and that is I *hate* to sweat. There, I said it out loud (well, you kind of have to take my word for that). Also, living in a warm climate and exercising makes excessive sweating even more prevalent. That's my excuse, anyway.

That doesn't mean I have not attempted exercise at all. I have tried various modes of exercise, but they just haven't been—um—sustainable.

In my mid-twenties, when I cared more about what I looked like, I not only had a gym membership but also used to do exercises at home every morning—for at least a few months, anyway. I guess I just got over that phase.

I even did a couple of charity ten-kilometre walks with a dear friend, followed by breakfast at the Pancake Parlour to celebrate our accomplishment because … well, we deserved it.

A handful of times, I have tried yoga classes, but found that, due to something to do with my anatomy I am guessing, I cannot lie flat on a floor. My back does simply not like it one bit.

I also find it extremely hard to relax. At the yoga classes I did attend, I'd contort my body into poses with curious names like *'downward facing dog'*, *'cow face'* (you can google it, I didn't make that one up) and *'big toe facing'* pose. This was usually followed by a lying-down relaxing meditation of some kind. I even recall hearing some people near me softly snoring, they were so relaxed.

Me, of course not! The way my mind works, I lay there going through what I needed to get at the supermarket on the way home or some such inane thought, whilst praying my stomach didn't grumble loudly enough for everyone to hear it. Although not so relaxing for me, I do appreciate the concept of it.

Another barrier to my participation in exercise of any form is my absolute inability to follow instructions, combined with my rather embarrassing lack of co-ordination.

I have always loved watching people ballroom dance and wished I had that ability. I even convinced Mr MICDL to attend a dancing lesson before our wedding in the vain hope I could possess that skill, too, and be whirled around the dance floor for our first bride and groom dance. It was meant to be a *'beginner's class'*, or so the ad professed, but I was gipped! We got there and all the people in the class had clearly attended the Arthur Murray School of Dancing or some such like, twirling around the room, proudly showing off their dancing prowess.

I have never felt so uncomfortable in my whole life, especially when we had to go round in a circle and change partners constantly. I don't know how many feet I trod on that night or how many eyebrows were raised at me. I felt like a baby elephant and, when it got to the coffee break time, I grabbed our things faster than you could say *'get me the hell out of here'* and ushered us out the door, never to return. You couldn't have paid me enough to do the second half of that so-called *'beginner's lesson'*. I felt like putting in a complaint about false advertising!

My partner, though, enjoyed it and must have possessed a left and a right foot, unlike like my two left ones. I must say, it was traumatising. So, I guess I will remain a wallflower, stuck watching from the sidelines forever more.

My understanding of how I need to keep some semblance of fitness is never lost on me, despite my previous trauma.

There was the time I bought a swim pass to attend an aqua-aerobics program. It was held on a morning during the week, so I thought that shouldn't be too bad, but how wrong I was once again! It was full of older ladies who obviously made it their weekly social *'chit-chat and catch up'* time. They sounded like a gaggle of geese. They were so loud, I couldn't hear what the aerobics instructor was yelling out on the edge of the pool as she threw her arms and legs about demonstrating the exercises.

The first time I attended, one woman (let's just call her 'Barbara') came up to me and in a bossy voice told me I was *'standing in Brenda's spot'* and needed to move. What the hell? I couldn't see any cross marks on the bottom of the pool designating Brenda's spot. I felt like hitting her over the head with my pool noodle!

To top it off, I'd forgotten my earlier experience of aqua-aerobics in my twenties. For some unknown reason, as soon as I try to exercise in the water, my feet instantly cramp up and I have to hop around in excruciating pain from one foot to the other, to try to 'de-cramp' them. Hence, after about three classes, that was that for me and my re-attempt at aqua-aerobics, and I forfeited my pool pass.

Lesson learnt. Don't buy passes or memberships to anything until you test drive them first. I feel like one of my purposes in life is to share this wisdom with whoever needs to hear it.

My final attempt at overcoming my exercise aversion was a few years ago when I attempted Zumba classes. I had watched a couple of YouTube lessons in the safety of my lounge room and thought maybe I could get the hang of it (delusional though I was). Even though I was sceptical about the following instructions bit (as previously explained), my thoughtful two-legged daughter must have felt sorry for me and sent me a link to a Zumba class in my local area, aptly named *'Zumba for the Unco'* (she explained it was short for *'uncoordinated'*).

Of course, it may just be me again (highly likely), but I find it impossible to watch someone demonstrate dance or exercise moves whilst I am supposed to be learning and undertaking said moves. To me, it is like attempting something whilst looking in a mirror and everything is back to front—right is left, left is right, you get the picture. (This could be connected to the same gene I am missing, as referred to previously, regarding parallel parking, folding a fitted sheet and also putting a pizza lid back on properly). I mean, I do try. You have to give me that.

Being the *'newbie'*, lots of nice ladies made reassuring comments to me upon seeing how uncoordinated I was, such as, *'It doesn't matter. Don't worry, love, I felt that way too when I started. You'll pick it up.'* I felt like a baby learning to walk for the first time and failing miserably. Also, I felt like I was going to have a heart attack, and there was much sweating involved (yuck).

Hence, Zumba participation probably only lasted about six weeks before I threw my hands up in the air and admitted defeat. There are just some things my body is not meant to do. That was my foray into *'Zumba for the Unco'*. Obviously, I need *'Zumba for the Incredibly Unco 10X on Steroids.'*

Maybe, one day, a form of exercise I can master will make itself known to me. Until then, I am stuck with walking. At least I can't get that wrong!

Actual picture of me in my favourite pyjama top and life motto.

Mr and Mrs MICDL's excellent adventure – Part One: Planes, trains and automobiles

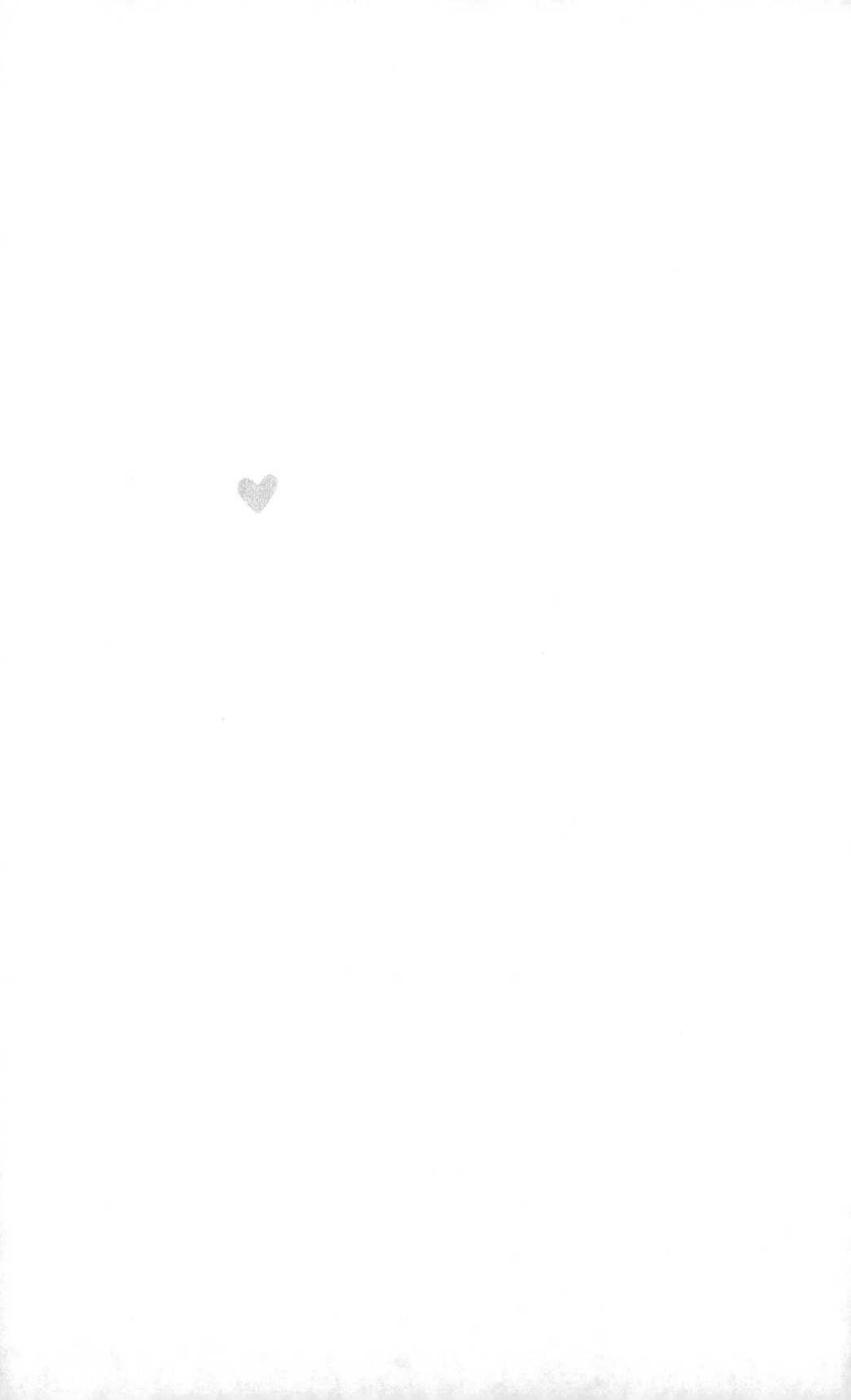

At the ripe old ages of sixty-four and fifty-nine respectively (I can't believe I said my age out loud—once again, you have to take my word for it!), Mr MICDL and I decided to head off on our first jaunt across the world to Europe.

I have to say I was a tad taken aback when I approached Mr MICDL suggesting this last moment idea. I knew his great dislike of flying long distances, due to being confined, becoming bored and unable to sit in one spot for more than ten minutes, and also, I guess, to be quite honest, not always being that fond of a lot of the human race. But, nevertheless, he agreed readily to the idea.

So, with less than six weeks to go before lift-off, we began interrogating Mr Google, before deciding it was all too hard to organise it ourselves and headed off to our local travel agent to book our trip.

Fast forward to the week before lift-off and, of course, we have the obligatory packing of the suitcases. What does one pack for this sort of adventure? Of course, too many clothes for the wrong weather that I will never end up wearing. Isn't that just what one does? It is necessary to pack something comfortable to wear on long flights, including, of course, compression stockings for our swelling aged legs, some sun frocks for warmer weather (for me only, Mr MICDL prefers shorts, although he has got the legs to get away with a frock, just saying!), something for cooler weather, something fancy, in case we go somewhere fancy, etc.

Before long, my suitcase looked like I had packed for the whole family, for six months, for every climate. Of course, necessary steps needed to be taken, including emptying everything out on the spare bed, counting outfits, weighing the suitcase and receiving stern looks from Mr MICDL, who was quite happy to travel with only a backpack. Who does that for nearly a month away in a foreign country? WTF!

Airports—oh my!

It's been a long time since I travelled overseas, and how times have changed at airports with all this digital business. Scan this, stand here on those footprints, hold your arms up out to the side, look at this light. I felt like a criminal and instantly guilty, kind of like when you see a police car next to you in traffic, even when you've done nothing wrong. The most criminal thing I have probably ever done in my life was to steal my neighbour's bundle of junk mail catalogues one time when my mailbox got overlooked. Don't judge me. I love my junk mail. How else can I keep up with what's going on in the world of retail?

Add into that post-nine-eleven, post-COVID and (by the way, I swear I am not exaggerating here, I have witnesses to this) I am *always* the person who gets pulled aside after going through security to be checked for drugs, explosives, you name it. I try not to take it too personally. I realise they have to reach their quota.

After being herded like a group of cattle through all the different checkpoints, being yelled at by some guy on the security checkpoint for taking my laptop out of my carry-on bag when I wasn't meant to (who knew?), we headed towards our plane.

Trains, planes and automobiles ...

Our first flight from Australia to Dubai was over fourteen hours. I knew how Mr MICDL struggled with anything longer than half an hour sitting in one spot. I also knew we couldn't justify the price of a small car to fly business or first class. Thankfully, our travel agent suggested we spend a little extra to get the extra-legroom seats.

It was well worth being able to stretch our legs, but it came with its own specific set of challenges. Mr MICDL had a grizzle when he realised this meant we didn't have a window to gaze out of, although to be honest, with fourteen hours up in the air there wasn't that much to look at, especially on a night flight.

Also, for some inexplicable reason, our entertainment device thingy didn't work, and despite alerting our trusty flight attendant, it remained that way for the entire fourteen hours. Mr MICDL ... not happy, Jan (remember, Mr MICDL glass half-empty, me glass half-full).

The other strange phenomenon about this extra legroom scenario is that we were next to one of the blocks of toilets. On the one hand, it was convenient to be that close to the amenities, but it didn't take us long to realise it certainly had its own particular downfalls, especially when the queue kept increasing and encroaching upon our *'extra leg room'*.

Not only did some people seem oblivious to our outstretched legs, but another strange bunch of people decided the space in front of us was the perfect spot to limber up from the long flight and do some calisthenics or star jumps. Numerous times, I found myself the victim of stray arms and legs being flung around and having to bring my knees up to my chest and hands over my head, to escape being knocked out by flailing limbs.

Ever heard of personal space, people? I think next time I will need to erect a barrier made up of pillows and blankets to clearly denote my *'extra leg room'* perimeter.

Airplane food is, of course, notoriously a gamble. Sometimes it can be pretty good and at other times, it may resemble hospital food, depending on which airline you fly. I don't know how they fit so many items on the small tray, each with its own respective spot. I always find myself juggling things and never being able to get everything back in its proper home, which is quite frustrating (hang on, I think some of Mr MICDL's traits must be rubbing off on me after all these years). Also, trying to rip the coverings off those little cups of juice can be particularly perilous, especially when turbulence is added into the mix.

It's a lot of pressure, and kind of reminds me of being at the checkout of an Aldi supermarket, trying to stuff everything into my shopping bags, while the cashier is scanning them at a rate of knots, simultaneously fumbling around to retrieve my credit card and pay, whilst the patrons behind me are glaring at me to hurry up. What's the rush, people?

(Sorry, I got distracted for a moment. Back to airline food). On this particular flight, the less than enthusiastic cabin crew reached our row with dinner and just said, *'chicken or beef'*. Chicken or beef what? Curry, roast, surprise? I'm not a mind reader, just saying.

After a while, you do tend to get a bit over the food. I don't usually eat meals like that at home, so I found the most appetising and fulfilling thing for me to eat were the cheese and crackers. However, at one point in the journey another strange moment occurred (maybe it's the altitude?). I was looking forward to relishing my final piece of cheese on cracker when, shut the front door, the last cracker mysteriously vanished! What the hell?

After searching everywhere, standing up, looking under the seat and peering suspiciously at the passenger next to me, I could not find it. Mr MICDL said, *'you probably ate it'*, to which he received a death stare back. I think I would know if I had done that, okay? To this very day, this remains, *'The Case of the Missing Cracker'*, never to be solved.

The eagle has landed

First stop in Mr and Mrs MICDL's big adventure was Dubai Airport. If you haven't been to Dubai Airport, it is kind of hard to put it into words. It is more like another world than just an airport. Having somehow managed to work out how to get our bags from the literally hundreds of baggage carousels (no exaggeration), the next challenge for this trusty duo was to proceed to customs.

You wouldn't think it would be that hard, would you? Well, for us, alas, it was just a smidge difficult. Even though there were signs in English, the description of which desk was for which type of passenger, being residents or non-residents, was less than clear. After asking, I exaggerate not, six different official-looking people, who each directed us to a different section, including one yelling at us in I-am-not-sure-what language whilst gesticulating angrily, somehow, we finally managed to get to the right desk, feeling somewhat like we were criminals and on the FBI's most wanted list.

So, following the first of our many airport *'incidents'*, and perhaps highlighting our lack of worldliness, Mr and Mrs MICDL's excellent adventure began! Our magical trip took us to Dubai, parts of Italy and Croatia, and opened our eyes to so many wonderful, beautiful and also a few somewhat strange customs, as highlighted below.

Flush and repeat ...

Finding bathrooms in Europe, as some of you may know, is a bit more challenging than Down Under where we live. Sadly, and maybe again, because of our age, it is a top priority while travelling. We do tend to take a lot for granted, but it is not until we are exposed to different countries and cultures that we realise how lucky we are living here. We had been forewarned about the lack of free or even public washroom facilities, so we thought we were well prepared—well, sort of anyway.

This daily scenario reminded me of when Miss MICDL was young. I would always say to her, whenever we were going out or if we were somewhere with facilities, *'Do you need to go?'* This seemed to be a constant phrase between Mr MICDL and moi on our travels.

One practice was to enter an eating establishment or bar and purchase something, which in itself was not such a bad idea, especially in the balmy weather conditions, so we could have access to the facilities. I must say, it's not a terrible way to prop up your takings if you are a restaurant, and it also gave us time to stop, relax and take in our surroundings. So, win-win!

One embarrassing incident which occurred in Italy, was, of course, no surprise, to yours truly. Whilst trying to decipher the pictures on the bathroom doors (remember my dislike of and laziness about taking out and putting on my glasses), I just gave them a cursory glance, pushed one of them open and entered. It was not until I exited that Mr MICDL, who was standing outside waiting for me, gave me an odd look, as well as the gentleman standing next to him. It seems because of my rapidly failing eyesight and stubbornness not to wear my glasses, that this *'Signora'* had just entered and exited the *'Signores*'! Mama Mia—how embarrassing!

The other challenging thing about travelling is trying to figure out how the *'equipment'* works in restrooms at hotels and airports. In one establishment, I entered the toilet cubicle, did what I needed to do, and as I stood up, the toilet magically flushed with such noise and vigour, I nearly fell over and hit my head on the cubicle door because it gave me such a fright.

Then there are the sinks for washing one's hands. Each one seems to hold a different mystery, testing my powers of detection. *Okay, how does this one work?* I think, as I wave my hands underneath the tap, over and around it, trying to release the water. I must look like I'm trying to perform a magic trick in front of the other occupants. But hey, if they are going to employ these special techniques, it would be handy if there was a *'How-To'* sign demonstrating said technique for those of us who have obviously led a sheltered life!

In one restaurant, we were enjoying a meal and I decided, now being a *'seasoned traveller'*, it would be a good idea to use the restroom before we left. I entered, locked the door and all of a sudden the light went out. So, there I was, in total darkness, feeling around the walls for a light switch. As I have no sense of direction or powers of observation (ask my husband), I didn't even know which way I was facing. If there was a camera in there (perish the thought), it would have looked like I was playing blind man's bluff.

Somehow, I'm not quite sure how, I managed to stumble my way through, and thank God, I found the door handle. I never did work out where that light switch was, though. I also found out when I rejoined my travelling party that apparently I was not the only one who experienced this *'black out'* situation. All I can say is that someone who works there must be having a good old giggle whenever they see an unsuspecting tourist stumble out the door looking flustered and harangued. Not really living a *'dolce vita'* moment!

The mystery of …

I always like to look for the quirky, funny side of things in life. I don't know where this particular part of my make up comes from, but I am fully embracing it. At this point in my life, I truly don't care what others think, possibly that I am a bit dotty, but so what! I like to have adventures. It makes life more interesting.

I had more than a couple of mysteries during our sojourn. I have already mentioned the *'Mystery of the Missing Cracker on the Plane'*. Now I will share another couple of my *'mystery'* moments with you!

The mystery of the one slipper
When we arrived at our destination in Croatia, on a beautiful island called Lopud Island, we were directed to our hotel

room. As it was rather late at night, we didn't get to check out much on the way. The next morning, we were waiting for the lift to go down to breakfast, which was situated next to a glass door leading to a small balcony. As I peered through the door to check out the beautiful view, I noticed one lonely-looking, white towelling slipper. You know, the ones that come with the room that you flip-flop around in?

Hmm, I thought, *that's a bit odd. Why only one? Was someone hobbling around their suite with one solitary slipper? Why is this so?* Every day, as we were travelling to and from our room, I glanced out at that slipper. *What's its story? Who does it belong to? Are they looking for it?* So many thoughts, I needed to get to the bottom of it (being dramatic again, of course, is in my DNA).

Finally, on the last day and as we were leaving, waiting to take our bags downstairs, I took a last glance through that door and voila, the slipper was gone! *Where? Who took it?* I will never know the answer to this mystery, and I guess I will have to live with that uncertainty forever.

The mystery of the sisterhood of the travelling underpants
As you may know if you are a seasoned globetrotter like me (not), it is usually necessary to handwash some smaller items whilst you are travelling, or you may find yourself running short of the essentials and unmentionables. One balmy morning staying on our island paradise in Croatia, I decided to handwash some items and, as we had a lovely balcony outside our room, I thought it would be the perfect place to hang my knickers out to dry.

Little did I know that during the day the breeze picked up. Little, also, did I know, that said breeze gently picked up a pair of my knickers and spirited them over to land on my next-door neighbour's balcony where, I gather, they were met with a little surprise when they opened their balcony door to check out the sunset.

Luckily, the neighbour happened to be one of our dear travelling companions. She returned them to my husband, I'm sure with a little grin on her face, accompanied by a chuckle at the circumstances. Things like this just seem to happen to me. I'm not sure why. Maybe so I can document them here, just like this, and have a good chuckle at myself!

Funny signs

I am not the world's best photographer (my daughter will attest to this) and have to admit when I looked back at the slew of photos I took on our trip, quite a few had a stray finger or thumb over part of the lens. I had no idea what many of the photos were of, and also, there seemed to be an inordinate number of photos and videos of my feet. But, hey, at least I try, okay? While most people are snapping away at the amazing scenery of Italy and Croatia, our two destinations, such as the row upon row of beautiful old buildings and cathedrals, breathtaking views and artworks, I was somehow drawn to the not so usual, the quirky, the odd. Like attracts like, right? I thought I would include a few of my snaps here with you, my dear reader, as it may be the only time they see the light of day again, and I want to share my photography prowess with the world somehow.

Bit late for that!

Another mystery! Where did it go?

When in Rome!

I could write so much about this amazing, once in a lifetime experience that Mr MICDL and I had the opportunity to enjoy, and all the laughs we experienced along the way. I could talk more about the food, the people we met, the treasures we saw, but I think one of the things I enjoyed most about it and that I will always remember, is the opportunity to experience this with Mr MICDL and see the smile on his face and the lightness in his step. Arrivederci, Italy and ciao for now—we will return!

Mr and Mrs MICDL's excellent adventure – Part Two: Men are from Venus, women are from Mars

There is something about me and a sense of direction ... I have none. This is amplified when I am in the presence of Mr MICDL even more. Whilst we recently traversed the thronging crowds and streets of Italy in the end-of-summer heat, it was he who led the way and got us to our next destination. Well, most of the time, anyway.

'The sun is over there, so that must be north', he proudly stated. Huh? Is that left or right? Don't come at me with this north, south, east or west stuff, buddy. Being a person with zero sense of direction, that means zippo to me.

'Let's just have a short walk today after all the walking we did yesterday,' he said. 'I read about an amazing palace and garden that is meant to be around here, where you get a view across the whole of Florence. Do you want to have a look? I don't think it's that far.'

Little did I know what was in store for us when I uttered the simple two words, 'Yes, sure.'

What is it with men and using maps (the same as instruction manuals)? I wouldn't think any less of him if he used a map, especially when we are in a foreign place neither of us have been to before. Is it meant to be sapping of masculine energy? Do men think it turns women off?

To all the men out there reading this (though probably none), that is far from the truth. It is actually quite attractive to women for men to use a map and instruction manuals. It means we get where we want to go in a timely manner and get things working the way they are supposed to. Win-win!

'Let's go up this street', he said, pointing to a road I can only describe as terrain where mountain goats hang out. Walking up the steep cobblestone road, we passed car after car parked on a gravity-defying slope (with me silently praying that they had good handbrakes). Frequent vehicles whizzed past us, up and down the road, which was so narrow we had to press ourselves against the side of buildings to let them pass.

We also passed many other seemingly displaced and disoriented tourists going either way up or down the steep street, wiping sweat off their brows and panting heavily. Some even stopped to ask us directions—misguided souls, they were!

'Are you sure this is the right way?' I managed to blurt out, whilst simultaneously gasping for breath.

'Well, the sun is over there, so it must be,' he responded.

Are you kidding me? That old chestnut again?

While we stopped for Mr MICDL to reorientate himself with the sun, and me to regain my breath, fruitlessly trying to mop up the ever-accumulating stream of sweat, a few other lost tourists came up to discuss this seemingly hard to locate Utopia up the top of the hill. Most of them, however, had their phones out trying to find it with something you may all have heard of, *'Google Maps'*. Not *my* trusty companion, though. He was going to rely on his orienteering skills, apparently learnt in his childhood long, long ago.

I suggested to him so many times that day to look up this elusive landmark on the phone, I was beginning to sound like a parrot. I was becoming annoying even to myself! Clearly, he didn't have his listening ears on either, as my suggestion was steadfastly ignored.

About an hour or more later, after seemingly walking in steep circles up and down random streets (because the sun told him to), we stumbled upon the garden and yes, I will admit it was an amazing sight. We dragged our sweaty bodies and tired feet up more steps to admire the view and took copious photos. We were glad we had the opportunity to see the majestic city of Florence in all its glory.

However, after we were all done, another dilemma seemed to present itself now ... we had to get down the hill again. Mamma Mia!

Beautiful Florence—actual photo taken by moi!
Not bad, huh?

Thelma and Louise (AKA Daisy and Maggie)

As they have a starring role in the title of these musings, it would be remiss of me if my four-legged foofy daughters (affectionately known as *'The Girls'*) did not have their own chapter of musings dedicated to them. Their foibles, idiosyncrasies and, most importantly, the way they bring so much joy to me, my family and everyone around them.

Writing this, I was contemplating back to when each *'girl'* came into my life, and what was going on with me at that particular time.

Daisy Girl

When my precious Daisy, the *'older sister'* (although sometimes I think she has more of an air of a *'spinster aunt'* about her) came into my life over fifteen years ago, the Universe in its innate wisdom decided to give her the role of *'the peacekeeper'*. She helped heal the slightly fractured relationship between my two-legged teenage daughter (Miss Puberty Blues) and her stepdad (Mr MICDL) and put the pieces of our dear family back together again.

I had been scanning the local animal sanctuary website looking for the *'right'* pup to join our family, unbeknownst to my two-legged daughter but beknownst to Mr MICDL, although I have to say he was less than enthusiastic about the whole idea. I don't know why, but I had this overwhelming urge to bring a dog into the situation. I guess it was what you might call a *'knowing'* that this was the right decision to make for all of us.

Finally, one Saturday morning, after weeks of pouring over the animal sanctuary website, I saw a dog who looked sweet, not too big and would suit our home and garden environment. Off to the sanctuary I went on a mission, taking with me a cane washing basket and a blanket, thinking I would be bringing home this particular dog that day (I'll call her Ruby to make it easier).

As the Universe had other plans and always knows what is best for us, when I got there and saw Ruby, I just didn't feel the connection. Plenty of people were standing around the enclosure oohing and aahing over her, so I was happy in the knowing that she would be going home with a new family that day.

At this exact moment, out of the corner of my eye, I saw this little grey and white fluffy dog, looking a little worse for wear, and my heart jumped into my throat. *That's her! She's the one!*

I don't think I've ever run so fast (I even impressed myself!), as I made a mad dash over to her enclosure. In fact, if anyone had got in my way, I think I probably would have pushed or knocked them over, the feeling was so intense. When I reached her enclosure and looked into those big, sad brown eyes, I instantly knew she would be coming home to join our family.

I grabbed the nearest volunteer I could, and together we ventured into the enclosure. They explained she had only arrived the day before from another animal sanctuary up north. They had no idea about her background or why she was surrendered, but she was extremely timid and scared. The poor darling hid under a chair and shook, and that was it for me. There was no going back.

After we had done all the paperwork, another lovely volunteer carried her out to my car, but clearly this little ball of fluff did not enjoy being carried at all. She scampered up his body like a cat, scratching him to bits in the process. He placed her in the washing basket next to me and she shook all the way home. I drove with one hand on the wheel and the other gently stroking and reassuring her that she would be safe now and loved. I promised her that.

When I arrived home, it was around 11.00 am and, like many teenagers I'm sure, on a Saturday morning, Miss MICDL was still ensconced in her bedroom lying in. I knocked on the door and asked, 'Can I come in? I have something to show you'

I heard a muffled groan in response. Taking that as an affirmative (I spoke teenager), I opened the door holding the washing basket with that little ball of fluff inside.

When I said, 'Look what I've got!', Miss MICDL sat bolt upright in her bed, the pure delight on her face one memory I'll never forget.

'Mum, you are so random!' she said to me, and that is where our love story with Daisy began.

I was right. Daisy had magical powers that brought the two of my most-loved human beings back together again, through their mutual care and love of her. I don't know how I knew, but I just knew, and I am forever grateful that this healed the relationship between Miss and Mr MICDL, and now they are both each other's biggest supporters.

For some inexplicable reason, though, this gorgeous creature had been named *'Bubbles'*. Don't know what that was all about, but it was definitely the first thing to change! I can't remember exactly how we came up with the name *'Daisy'*, but that is and will always remain her name, although she does have a few pseudonyms of her own that have crept in over the years, such as *'Lazy Daisy'*, *'Crazy Daisy'*, *'Miss Daisy Bear'* and recently I have been calling her *'Little Chicken'*.

Daisy was more like a cat than a dog, maybe due to whatever mistreatment she had sadly been exposed to, or, as Miss MICDL called her, *'cat-dog'*. She didn't like being picked up, was definitely not a lap dog, didn't like being patted, but rather would tell you she wanted some affection by coming up to you and gently tapping you with her paw. We loved and accepted her exactly as she was—perfect in our eyes.

Daisy also had special powers. When my dear dad was very ill in hospital and my mother came to stay for a time, Daisy lay outside her bedroom door at night as though she was protecting her. My mum and Daisy had a special connection, too.

Honestly, what a gift this beautiful dog has been to our lives. We have been so truly blessed. We love you more than sunshine, Daisy Girl …

Maggie Bear

At the time this goofy, lovable girl came into our life, I told my husband I thought Daisy was lonely and needed company. This wasn't exactly the truth now when I look back. She was purely brought into our family because, again, the Universe in her wisdom, knew I needed her to help with the healing of my own heart and soul.

Leading up to Maggie becoming part of the family, I had gone through what I can only describe as a nervous breakdown due to several life issues, including the loss of my darling dad, running my own business and, at the same time, running myself into the ground.

I can't even remember how I found Maggie, but I have never regretted it for one second, although to this day, I think Daisy is still miffed about it and simply *'tolerates'* her younger sister. To the contrary, Maggie absolutely adores her older sister, although is insanely jealous of any attention that Daisy receives (or anyone else, for that matter) which takes away attention from her. This *'girl'* suffers from serious FOMO!

Maggie also can't be left alone for a second at feeding or treat time. As soon as our backs are turned, she pushes Miss Daisy out of the way with her big, boofy head and gobbles up both their meals. No boundaries, this girl!

Darling Maggie, aka *'Miss Maggie Bear'*, *'Big Bottomed Girl'*, *'Needy is her Middle Name'* and, finally, *'Big Chicken'*. Maggie has now been part of the MICDL crew for nearly ten years, and I love that *'The Girls'* are growing old together. She is kooky, cheeky, needy, has a monster appetite, will steal the food out of her sister's mouth, loves sitting on my lap (all twenty-eight kilograms of her) and snores like a grown man with sleep apnoea, but I wouldn't have her any other way!

I will always treasure the moments I have shared with these gorgeous creatures who bring me such joy and laughter, are so patient with me as I chew their ear off with my nonsensical chatter, are wonderful to hug and always happy to see me. Thank you to the Universe in all your wisdom for granting me this amazing opportunity to be their human mother. It is a priceless one for which I will be forever grateful.

All my 'Girls'

Men-o-pause (OR It's getting hot in here!)

Mother Nature, what would we do without her? (Well, I guess if you want to get technical, we wouldn't be here, would we!)

She must be a female, I'm guessing, or why would she be called *'Mother'*, but I would like to speak to someone in management in the MN crew about a certain matter. Why did she feel that the members of the female race needed to take on so much of the *'work'* in the battle of the sexes?

Now don't get me wrong, I wouldn't trade being a female for anything. The biggest gift for me personally was being able to bring my beautiful daughter into the world, but sometimes it does feel like we got the short end of the stick, so to speak.

Up until middle-age, it didn't seem to be such an issue being a member of the *'fairer'* sex, but then, out of the blue—kapow, bam, WTF! Out of the shadows, where it had been lurking, biding its time, came menopause or, as whispered in hushed tones by our mothers back in the day, *'the change of life'*.

I was thinking the other day when I decided to put pen to paper about this topic, what a strange word *'menopause'* is and also what a strange term *'the change of life'* is. The

Oxford Dictionary definition of *'men-o-pause'* is *'the time during which a woman gradually stops menstruating, usually at around the age of fifty.'*

So, looking at this definition, it made me wonder. What's the *'pause'* bit got to do with it? It's over, full stop. Why is it not *'meno-stop'* or *'meno-cease'*? It doesn't make sense to me, just saying, and then *'the change of life'* bit. What are we changing from and to?

Also, once I started thinking about this subject, many other questions were raised. Maybe you or someone you know have had the same thoughts (don't be surprised if you or they haven't, because as stated previously, my mind works in a particularly unique and odd way sometimes). My top thought was … drumroll please …

If women experience Men-o-Pause, do men experience Women-o-Pause?

Sorry, I know that was a bit corny. I just can't help myself sometimes!

From my research, I have read that some women, thankfully, sail through this phase of life. I'm glad to hear that. As luck would have it, I am not one of those chosen few. (Still paying off the debt from having been the naughty rebel in my earlier life is what I'm thinking).

I have detailed below a few situations I have experienced during this stage of my life. Looking back, I'm not quite sure when I first began noticing some of these. They seem to have insidiously developed over a few years, then really begun to make their presence felt.

1. It's getting hot in here!

I guess for many women (including myself), the first symptom of menopause we may notice is the change in our body temperature regulation. I refer to it as having my own *'temperature zone'*. It may be twenty-two degrees Celsius in the location I am at, but it can be at least thirty-five degrees in my *'zone'*. This phenomenon could appear during the night in bed or during the day. It doesn't care, but boy, it certainly makes itself known.

Often, I am sitting in my lounge room watching TV when I utter the words, *'Is it hot in here or just me?'* Upon regularly asking this question and seeing both Mr MICDL and Miss MICDL roll their eyes and answer in a bored, monotone voice, *'It's just you'*, I learnt pretty quickly it was probably fruitless to ask them and expect a different response.

So, how does this affect you when it occurs at night? I can only go by my own history, and that of my close friends and sister. For me, it involves not knowing what to wear to bed and not knowing what sort of covering to have over me in bed. I have alluded to this in prior chapters (please see Chapters 7 and 11).

The night may play out like this. For example, on a cool evening, it may seem sensible to wear warmer PJs with legs or place a warmer blanket or quilt on the bed. Into bed I hop, feeling comfortable and snuggling into the pillow (or perhaps Mr MICDL, if he's lucky). Sometime during the night, I may suddenly awaken, feeling like I am sleeping on an electric blanket set to the hottest setting.

I then may realise that my sleepwear is stuck to my skin,

my hair is wet and I am drenched in sweat. Not the most pleasant feeling, let me tell you. Meanwhile, Mr MICDL is dreaming sweet dreams in the land of nod, complete with nose whistle and snoring, while I am lying there feeling like Mount Vesuvius about to erupt.

It's kind of hard to go back to sleep when I am feeling this way, so this usually results in throwing off some or all of the covers, thrusting out a stray arm or leg to catch some cool air and trying as best as possible to grab a few more hours (or, in my case, minutes) sleep. This is usually when the *'rotisserie chicken manoeuvre'* also comes into play (please refer to Chapters 1 and 11).

The other option is to get up, change clothes, splash water on yourself and perhaps head to the spare room (see previous musing in Chapter 11) which may probably also result in a little sleep being achieved. Sigh …

My best friend has decided for her own sanity, and desire to get some sleep, that she requires the overhead fan plus an upright fan focused on her 365 days of the year. Unfortunately, I don't think that Mr MICDL would be on board with that request due to his own sleep challenges (as alluded to previously).

However, this symptom of menopause can also strike at the most inconvenient and inappropriate times. Many a time I have been at our local shopping centre, maybe spending a few hours browsing, when I have been overcome by an overwhelming feeling which I can only describe as akin to self-combustion. It is usually in a store where there are many bright lights, which seem to produce an inordinate amount of heat. I kid you not, it has taken all my strength on such occasions not to rip off all my clothes, whilst simultaneously gasping for breath and trying not to pass out.

As such, I have learnt that the best approach for a menopausal woman who experiences this symptom is to dress is in layers, especially in the colder months, and to carry a bottle of water at all times. I am happy to pass on my wisdom in this matter.

2. What did I come into this room for again?

It's not only temperature regulation that seems affected for a lot of us. Other symptoms also arise, which can have a real impact on how we function during the day, at home and at work. I remember my older sister (who is quite a brainiac and knows a lot about a lot of different things) telling me that menopause affected her concentration. At that stage, I wasn't experiencing this, so thought I must have dodged that particular bullet. But alas, again, it was only temporary and into play it came.

So how does this impact me personally? Well, all my life I have been an avid reader. I remember as kids, we went to the library every week after school, and it was nothing for me to read around four or more books a week. This carried on throughout my teenage and adult life. For me, there was nothing better than getting lost in a book. I also found it a great way to get to sleep and often woke up in the morning still holding a book in my hand. (Pre-Mr MICDL of course. That wouldn't pass muster with our sleep challenges.)

Now I am lucky to get through reading one solitary page,

let alone an entire book. Even then, I may have to re-read it more than once for the information to sink in. I was hoping this would pass, and I could concentrate once again, but sadly, it's been quite a few years now. A number of unread books remain in my bookcase, and I glance at them with dismay in the vain hopes that one day my concentration will magically reappear.

It also has affected my word-finding ability. I was terrified I may be experiencing early dementia at the start, as I desperately and fruitlessly tried to find the word I was looking for. A typical conversation with Mr MICDL may go like this:

Me: 'I need to get one of those things when we go to the supermarket to make tonight's dinner.'

Mr MICDL: 'What thing? What are you talking about?'

Me: 'You know, they're brown and have bumpy skin and you have them with Mexican food.'

Mr MICDL: You mean an avocado? Why didn't you just say that?'

Well, duh, I would have if I could remember the word, wouldn't I! (I wouldn't say that out loud, I promise. That is a head conversation—I'm not a mean-spirited person).

It similarly affects my cognition in such a way that sometimes I am unable to make a decision. It could be as simple as what I want for lunch or what I want to wear. This debate in my head can go on for what seems like forever, until I make the decision or just give up because I'm over it, exhausted and just want to lie down and have a nanna nap.

Of course, as we advance in age, many of us have had the experience of going into a room to get something, and totally forgetting once we are there what it was we wanted. Yes, that also happens multiple times a week to me, made worse because we live in a two-storey house. Although, looking on the bright side, at least I am getting some exercise traipsing up and down the stairs. It's the only exercise I do get. (Please refer to Chapter 12 for this aspect of my existence).

3. It's all downhill from here

Apparently, as we get older and go through menopause, our bodies start to run out of vital stuff that impacts our different systems. In my research, I found an article that said there are thirty-four major symptoms of menopause. I looked at the first few and slammed my laptop shut in dismay. I don't think I need to scare myself any further. Also, I am worried I might develop some of these symptoms psychosomatically if I read too much about them. I'm a bit like that. Best not to consult Dr Google if you are like me.

But apparently, some of the more common physical effects of menopause may result in conditions such as osteoporosis (due to low calcium levels), low libido (reduced oestrogen), mood swings and mood changes, hair loss, sudden weight gain, the list goes on and on. Yippee … yeah, not.

One of the symptoms not listed amongst those thirty-four

was something I have experienced a lot lately, being leg and feet cramps at night in bed. These have hit me like a ton of bricks as recently as last night.

The situation usually plays out like this. I finally drift off to sleep with all my various challenges (heat, snoring, etc.) when I am abruptly awoken by searing, acute pain and stiffness in my lower limb. As much as I try to ignore it, this is impossible. Even the weight of a sheet on me is unbearable. Attempts at massaging it whilst lying there are usually fruitless. Eventually, I have to get up and hobble around the bedroom, whilst trying not to disturb my sleeping buddy, until the pain subsides. Then I attempt to get back to sleep again. Not the most pleasant of situations. You will understand if you have experienced this, I am sure.

The other thing that seems to happen to me at night is even more insomnia—like I need more of that! It seems impossible to switch my mind off, and as you may know from reading this, the things that cram my brain are usually of the nonsensical kind and useless. I have detailed these in Chapter 10, but again to refresh your memory, dear reader, some of these random thoughts consist of topics such as going through the plot of the show I watched prior to retiring to bed. I pick it to pieces, seeing all the holes in the plot. I consider *'vital'* questions such as whether a dog's front leg joint is called an elbow and the back leg joint a knee, and more. Honestly, some nights I would pay a million dollars just to sleep uninterrupted (if I had a million dollars, that is).

4. Midlife Puberty Blues

As a teenager, I remember making fun of my mother for crying at everything. Having never understood why she was like that, now as I look back, I realise it was around the time she was going through the *'change of life'* (for some weird reason I feel like I should whisper that). She also had a tendency to fly off the handle at the slightest thing. Unfortunately for us, most of it was aimed at my sister, me and my poor darling dad, the sweetest, softest man you could ever meet. As a young person watching this unfold, I'm afraid I used to blame my mum for being unreasonable and, well, sometimes just plain mean, but as a MICDL, I think I may finally get it.

I often describe this stage of my life as the *'Midlife Puberty Blues'*. Crying, well, what can I say, I have become my mother! Apart from sobbing my heart out in movies when I was younger such as *'Love Story'*, *'Sunshine'* and my all-time favourite *'Steel Magnolias'*, I never would have called myself a *'crier'*. However, this quickly changed when I found myself crying at everything I watched, including commercials on TV. I discovered it wasn't all bad, though. It's allowed me to release a lot through the tears, and I still carry on to this day when I am watching shows, or even hearing stories of people going through sad or tough times. (Sorry, Mum, I owe you another apology, xxx).

Even though most of this piece is written in a light-hearted manner, I guess what I really wanted to share is this is a time when your emotions can totally get the better of you. I actually went through what I can only describe as a nervous breakdown in my mid-fifties. It was due to a culmination of running my own business, working seven days a week, not being able to say no to my clients, my OCD tendencies to produce perfect work for them, all while pushing down chronic anxiety I never realised I had suffered from all my life.

At times, it can feel like you are going mad, and it can be very isolating. It can affect every aspect of your life, including your relationships. It's important to keep tabs on it, and I am a huge advocate of always reaching out for help and support when you need it. You don't need to carry this burden on your own. Someone is always there for you, and this is temporary.

Now, you may be thinking I have so far been simply focusing on the negative aspects of this stage of life we call menopause, and I guess you are correct. However, there are always two sides to a coin, so I will now focus on some of the more positive outcomes, because it also heralds a new phase in your life:

- No more periods. Yippee! Saving dollars and inconvenience.
- No more need for contraception once you are out the other side.
- Somehow you (or it could be just me) care less about what other people think of your appearance and what you wear. You may decide to wear leisure wear all day, every day. If you feel like it, just do it (That's a *hell yeah* from me!).

It is also a time for reflection, to take stock of all the life lessons and gifts you have experienced, the knowledge you have gained over this lifetime and have gratitude for making it this far and, most importantly, for the loved ones you have in your life.

I think Mother Nature is pretty smart, don't you? She reminds us of what is most important in this world we inhabit. Still, waiting for MN's management to get back to me, though. I reckon we could definitely make a few tweaks, don't you?

Afterword

Thank you, my dear reader. I guess if you are reading this section, you have made it through the somewhat bumpy and unique journey of my imagination. I hope you enjoyed the ride!

My hope is that this book will allow you to celebrate the wonderfulness of you, your own imagination, quirks, foibles and individual outlook on life, and maybe not take yourself and life too seriously. We are all unique, and I truly believe that our uniqueness should be celebrated.

My belief is that our ultimate goal of being here on this earth for the time that we are is to fully enjoy our lives. Not to compare ourselves to others, and not to simply reach for goals or attain *'things'* and then measure our *'successes'* by that.

Life is truly for living, so I encourage you to grasp onto whatever brings you that happiness and joy, and truly immerse yourself in it. As you do so, it miraculously allows your loved ones and others around you to experience the same feelings, kind of by osmosis. What a gift that is!

So, dear one, our time for now is over ... or is it? Watch this space!

Ciao for now!

Acknowledgements

It is my honour to acknowledge those who have loved, guided, inspired and supported me whilst this book came to be.

Once again, it has been such a gift and honour to have the incredible Natasha Gilmour of The Kind Press guide me through the journey of bringing this book to life. Thank you for believing in my vision to bring more light and laughter to the world and for joining me on this crazy rollercoaster ride! I could not have done it without your unwavering support and wisdom.

A ginormous thank you to the exceptionally talented and world-renowned illustrator, Gemma Correll, for so kindly illustrating my book cover. I have admired your work for years and feel such a strong connection to it (and to you!). I feel truly privileged that you said 'yes' when I approached you for this project—you captured me perfectly in a nutshell!

To my precious daughter Alex—I often wonder what it is like to have a mother like me?! Thank you, Poppet for your every present support and encouragement and most of all for just being you. You inspire me.

Thank you to all my friends who have joined me in my adventures over the years and laughed along with me. Laughter is so much more fun when it is shared, and I have been blessed to have the most wonderful friends in my life.

To my darling Mr MICDL—this book wouldn't be complete without you. Thank you for your endless patience, understanding, all the laughs we have shared and being the yin to my yang. You are a brave man, that's for sure!

To my darling four-legged fluffy daughters—Daisy and Maggie, thank you for choosing me to be your guardian. My life would have never been as full of so much love without you. Darling Daisy, I miss you every day my little koala bear. Sending you kisses over the Rainbow Bridge.

Finally, thank you to those who have chosen to pick up this book. May you be brave, take risks, laugh and forgive, never take yourself too seriously and most of all see yourself for the amazing person you are, perfectly imperfect like us all.

About the Author

Suzie de Jonge is a writer, devoted mother, quirky wife, and (of course) a crazy dog lover who lives by the philosophy, 'Life is a roller coaster, you may as well be along for the ride.' She's had a myriad of adventures as a professional in hospitality, HR, healthcare, entrepreneurship and life coaching. Eccentricity is her delight, and she's found her bliss in the little things.

Along her winding journey of self-discovery, Suzie revived her childhood passion for writing, publishing her debut novel, *The Untangling*, which was featured in *MiNDFOOD Magazine*. Her work also appears in *Unity: A Tapestry of Stories to Spark Belonging, Connection and Liberation*. Blending her love of comedy and serious reflection, Suzie has co-written a feature film script inspired by *The Untangling*—a dramedy exploring the complexities of sometimes-fraught parent-child relationships and finding peace within those relationships and ourselves.

suziedejonge.com.au